ALL OVER THE PLACE: A LIFE

All Over the Place: A Life

Ron Southerton

Valley Press

First published in 2013 by Valley Press
Woodend, The Crescent, Scarborough, YO11 2PW
www.valleypressuk.com

ISBN: 978-1-908853-25-7
Cat. no.: VP0032

A CIP record for this book is
available from the British Library

Printed and bound in Great Britain by
Imprint Digital, Upton Pyne, Exeter

Typeset in Palatino Linotype, 10pt on 12.

CONTENTS

CHRONOLOGY

1925	Born in Derby, 14 January
1936	Grammar school
1943	Technical College
1945	Army:

1946: Commissioned
1947: Egypt; Palestine
1948: Tripoli, Libya {1949: Marriage}
1950: Korea
1952: Petts Wood
1954: Swanage
1955: North Finchley
1956: Aden
1959: Arborfield

1960	Little Chalfont
1966	Finspång, Sweden
1971	Shearsby
1978	Baghdad, Iraq
1980 — ∞	Scarborough

For Betty, who makes my life worth while.

FOREWORD

It has been a privilege for me to write the Foreword to Ron's autobiography, for that is what this book surely is. He has been able to marshal his thoughts and to put them down in clear detail without undue padding. One might say typical of the engineering mind, but Ron is more than that, he is a literary engineer if that is not a contradiction in terms. Ron's life, which in time became so intrinsically interwoven with his wife Betty's, is a fast moving account of a purposeful, industrious, colourful, fascinating, inventive and at times exciting chronicle.

This is a book which will appeal to a wide range of ages and people. For those of us brought up through the 20th century it will be a nostalgic journey as we recall and empathise with those episodes in his childhood and adolescence so clearly explored. We may all say: 'Something like that happened to me when I was in …' We learn something of the fantasies that enabled him and his friends to explore their environment and hence enrich their lives in a way that today's children are unable to do, either because of suspicion of the strangers in their midst and their motives, or that they are caught up in the virtual reality games of the X-box and television screen that supply them with their kicks from an armchair. These, paradoxically, come from the inventive minds of the mechanic and the scientist in the technological world of which Ron is a part!

Here is a man who has been alert to the opportunities afforded him in life and has made the best of them. Ron is a breed apart, an assertive international technocrat whose knowledge, skills and sharp inventive mind have made him sought after by companies and businesses who recognized his talents, business acumen and literary ability; a wide spectrum of skills seldom found in one person. He has ability with languages, particularly with Swedish and French.

The Second World War had a profound impact on his life and his graphic description of the commencement of his military service is noted with some feeling. He rose to the rank of major in the regular army and he gives us further descriptions of his service in different parts of the world, including Israel in 1948, Libya in 1949, front-line duties in the Korean War in 1950 and finally Aden in 1957. With Ron's army duties it became up to the versatile and energetic Betty to make the arrangements for their wedding in All Saints, Mackworth, just outside Derby. After his unusual indulgence flight from his Libyan base to home Ron and Betty were married on 27 July 1949. Betty's introduction to married life in Tripoli provided her with a myriad of new and in some cases traumatic experiences, but she coped well with them with a mature resilience. These had a profound effect on her that enabled her to make the most of their experience of expatriate life later in Aden, Sweden and Iraq.

It is clear that Betty had to cope with another love – that of Ron's apparent obsession with things mechanical, from Centurion tanks in the Egyptian desert and the Korean paddy fields to steam locomotives in Nairobi and Doncaster, where he had the opportunity to ride the famous Mallard. Following his retirement from the army Ron worked for some time in London as a journal editor before accepting a post with a Swedish engineering firm. They lived in Sweden for five years. Like all of the posts he held this too required him to travel extensively including a fascinating journey through what was then the Eastern Bloc by car via East Berlin, Dresden and Prague en route to Brno in Czechoslovakia. A post with GEC took them from the Leicester area to Baghdad in Iraq where they lived for two years. In 1979 he resigned from GEC and in 1980 he and Betty moved to Scarborough where they continue to live peacefully, although talking to them both you do get that hint they would still like to be on board the life that has taken them to many parts of the world.

Ron is not one to shout his exploits from the rooftops, but maybe he should, because this is a fascinating story that many would find gripping and interesting. Of course, when asked his considered opinion about anything mechanical he will be only too pleased to give you the benefit of his wisdom and experience. One aspect of his life which must also be mentioned is his love of music and his ability as a musician, which is another string to his rather large bow.

This life story will provide any young aspiring engineer with encouragement and inspiration on how to develop a career in this field. In any event, enjoy what Ron has written; I certainly did.

The Reverend Richard Costin

PREFACE

The trouble with any 'my life' story, or autobiography if we want to be proper, is that it is full of I, me and my; that may be self-evident, but to me it also feels self-indulgent, which I cannot avoid. My problem in composing this personal tale has been one of memory, as I had kept no diaries which might have helped to bring back those distant days. On the other hand when writing I have found that a natural momentum seems to come into play, whereby to get into one little anecdote jogs the memory of something else not thought of until then.

I am privileged to have lived and worked all over the place, to have travelled to many countries both in my business world and as a tourist and to have met so many lovely people. Huge technological changes have occurred since the childhood days of my parents at the end of the Victorian era, yet the humanitarian, economic and political iniquities in the world refuse to be resolved. In this context, any one life story becomes insignificant outside a personal group of family, old friends and new friends; you, they, are the ones who matter to me. Our life in this universe lasts for but one moment in the infinity of time; it is a moment to treasure.

Enjoy these words, be reminded of any event where I have brushed against you and fill in the gaps where you will. I am indebted to my publisher Jamie McGarry of Valley Press for his guidance. I thank Kjell Lundin for his graphic design and linguistic expertise; Richard and Jill Costin and David and Hildegard Smart for their constructive textual advice; Richard again for his foreword; Dr Geoffrey Smith for his meticulous reading of the final MS; and my wife Betty for her infinite tolerance. All remaining mistakes are to my account.

Ron Southerton
Scarborough 2013

ORIGINS

'Go not forth hastily to strive, lest thou know not what to do in the end thereof.' – Proverbs 25:8

Family folklore always had it that my birth had been rather dramatic – for my mother, that is. She was in mortal danger when her second child was delivered at home with great difficulty on the 14th of January 1925. At first, all efforts were devoted to saving mother while I was temporarily consigned to the floor. Later they picked me up to discover that 'the little blighter's still alive!' Forcep marks were visible on my temples up to 40 years later.

The place was number 49 Jackson Street, Derby, a terraced house with a front door onto the pavement, coal cellar underneath and outside toilet at the back; all very typical of its day in an industrial city. An 'entry' or through passageway pierced the terrace blocks every fourth house. This tunnel ended in two wooden gates, each serving two houses, and each house had a garden no larger than five paces by eight enclosed by high brick walls. Coal was delivered straight from the street through a grating in the pavement under the front room window into the cellar below. There was gas lighting on the ground floor in the back room and front room only, a black-leaded grate with side oven in the back room, a shallow stone sink and copper in the scullery, and a tin bath hanging on the wall when not in use. No electricity, you will notice.

The house door led directly into the front room, from where a door connected to the kitchen via a narrow passageway which had a side door giving entrance to the dark cellar steps. The kitchen had a sash window overlooking the yard and a door into a scullery that projected down one side of the yard. Another door in the corner closed off the boxed-in staircase that climbed up steeply behind the fireplace. There was lino on the boarded floors, blue enamel candlesticks and candles only upstairs. No carpets.

This was the decade of the General Strike of 1926 and the Great Depression of 1929, hard times indeed for Britain. We lived in number 49 until I was nearly four years old. The family had arrived there from Birmingham a few years earlier. Father was a weighing machine fitter with Avery's Scales of Solihull who was transferred to Derby in about 1921 to become foreman manager of Avery's premises in Sadler Gate. He was promoted to the highest skilled grade of Adjuster-in-Charge in 1931.

At the time of my birth my brother Thomas Henry (Tom) was seven years old. He had been born in Birmingham, where our family links remained strong. On 22 February 1925 I was christened Ronald Clarence in St Saviour's Church, Lozells, a district of the inner city of Birmingham. The middle names of both Tom and me came from father: Henry and Clarence, one each. There were no other siblings.

Our neighbours sharing the same back yard were market traders George and Flo Warburton, affectionately known as big Warbo and little Warbo (although neither of them was above about 5ft 2in tall and my parents not much more). My best friend in those days was Kenny Roome, some months older than me, who lived in the end house of the terrace which had a driveway at the side. At the back stood his father's large tool shed, which became famous when at the age of three years or so Kenny and I found a tin of distemper and decorated the inside of the shed and most of ourselves as well.

I have two other memories of that street. One is the corner shop at the junction with Lynton Street, where mother would send me to buy household oddments such as replacement mantles (the delicate mesh elements for the gas lamps). On these expeditions I usually managed to beg a bag of pork scratchings, a great delicacy. The other memory is of that tunnel-like entry between the houses which I shot through on my three-wheeler out onto the pavement, much to the consternation of any ladies passing by; they had no right to get in the way of a trainee hooligan! I could do a wheelie without going on the road. This fiendish tricycle was a real chain-driven job with standard wheels and tyres, hardly a toy.

Before the age of four I started school at a C of E Practising College, a teacher training college. It stood in its own grounds 200 yards away via Drury Lane and across the nearby main Uttoxeter road into town. Strange to relate that many years later my eventual brother-in-law, Dennis, would marry a girl from Drury Lane, Doreen Mills, who later lived in Jackson Street opposite our number 49. Our family transport in those days was a motor bike and sidecar. One of the usual annual holidays was to the Wales coast. Mother held me on her lap in the sidecar while Tom rode on the pillion seat. A look at a map today will show what a tortuous journey that was; there were no dual carriageways or motorways then.

In May 1928 came the big family event: the wedding of mother's sister Dolly to Horace Light in Birmingham. The wedding photograph shows an innocent pageboy sitting hands on knees in the front row, looking as though he is on a potty. No prizes for guessing who he was! Sixty years later I had to give the speech at the diamond wedding party held in their house in Little Aston Park near Sutton Coldfield. On that occasion, a unique group photograph was taken of all eleven of distaff-side Grandma Deakin's grandchildren as adults, in descending order of age from Tom and me at one end down to cousin Pat and finally cousin Anne at the other. Aunt Lily, the youngest of the sisters, had six children, Aunt Dolly had three, and mother, the oldest, had just us two. There was our Uncle Tom, who was the oldest of Gran Deakin's children, but he had died before this anniversary.

In 1929 we moved house to number 53 Chain Lane, Derby, half way between Littleover and Mickleover. It was a narrow wandering lane connecting Burton Road to Uttoxeter Road, and probably considered quite an upmarket suburban area, though I was too young to make that sort of judgment. The bottom of our garden was not far from the outer reaches of the Mickleover golf links and there were plenty of big houses which took advantage of that prime situation. One of those houses was occupied by the Hulme family who ran Derby's posh wireless and gramophone shop at the top end of Sadler Gate, just below Lloyds Bank on the corner. On one occasion in 1937, or perhaps 1938, we kids peered through their front room window and saw a small working television set, flickering and blurred.

At the upper end of Chain Lane, towards Burton Road, the houses originally all had long front gardens and high hedges bordering the lane; I remember negotiating them in the dark when we kids went round singing Christmas carols in due season. Our end of Chain Lane was not in that class. We rented number 53 from Sam Hill, the town's leading scrap dealer, his father being of like name and business and well into property holdings. Sam lives on in memory for Betty and me through his gift of a half-dozen tea set of posy pattern Crown Derby for a wedding present. It supplemented the half set I had given Betty on her 21st birthday. This high quality china with its evocative memories of my home town survives, boosted by a few replacements. After we moved into Chain Lane, Sam Hill came to live in the last house in Corden Avenue, by the field. Later he moved to a bigger house in Station Road, Mickleover, not far from the railway station, now long gone. That house had a large orchard that provided an ideal training ground for young scrumpers, equipped with bicycles and saddle bags, who frequently needed a cure for stomach ache. The house also had very large lawns, which Sam cut by means of a sit-on mower, quite a fearsome clattering piece of machinery for its day.

To round off the Sam Hill story I have to think ahead to our family visits to beautiful Dovedale just north of Ashbourne, where I would scramble to the top of Thorpe Cloud and yodel my boy alto heart out, delighting in hearing the echoes rolling back down the valley. Whenever we went on holiday with Dolly, Horace, Sam Hill and families to the south coast, Sam insisted I ride in the back of his Ford Terraplane, a big open tourer, to entertain him with my yodelling party piece. The big V-8 could easily climb the one-in-two-and-a-half gradient out of Babbacombe beach, whereas Dad's passengers had to dismount while he crawled up in bottom gear, or even in reverse with Mum and Tom standing by to push.

Number 53 Chain Lane was a small three-bedroom semi with electric lighting and a gas cooker. An outside loo was built into the back of the house and there was another in the bathroom upstairs – such luxury! I don't think the outside loo got used for its intended purpose, but Dad screwed two pigtail hooks into the top of the door frame so that with the door open I could hang my swing on short ropes and practice self-destruction. The house had no hot water system as such, but in the bathroom was a huge gas-fired geyser, a copper cylinder suspended over the end of the bath which provided hot water for the weekly ritual. It was lit by a long taper and started up with an explosive whoomph. Despite the modern facilities, Dad continued to wash and shave in the kitchen as he had done at number 49. His shaving brush, soap and cut-throat razor lived on the kitchen window-sill, a practice he continued resolutely all his life.

I had the small back bedroom over the kitchen, once again with lino but with the luxury of a pegged rug on the floor by the bed. It was cold in bed, even with a stone hot-water bottle, and the only way to relieve the resulting chilblains was to lie in bed and pick bits of wallpaper off the wall for fun. When I was older I had a flat torch with a fish-eye lens at one end, probably given as a Christmas present, which simplified reading in bed. The other unusual feature of the house was the tight spiral staircase leading off the little straight hallway just inside the front door.

The houses opposite came to an end about three doors up, and the Warbos now lived in the end house next to the field. The bottom of their garden, in effect, backed on to Sam Hill's in Corden Avenue. Warbo ran a drapery stall in the Morledge, Derby's open-air market, and had the great luxury of a small driveway. Where a garage would stand, he had a large wooden shed, which he used for his drapery stocks and as a workshop, heated by a blue flame paraffin stove. I was fascinated by the aroma of hot paraffin fumes. George would stand at his bench puffing a pipe, cutting long straps of leather by hand into bootlaces to sell on his market stall. Their fierce wire-haired fox terrier, Spot, kept guard; he lived in an outdoor kennel. Later still, the Warbos bought a house and shop on Upper Boundary Road, not far from where I had been born.

My new best pal now was Nev Potter, who lived across the road with his mother and charming grandmother, Mrs Knowles. He was a year younger than me, but about one foot taller; we were to stay together throughout our teenage school years. Playing in the fields around us was no problem then, as Corden Avenue was a cul-de-sac which did not connect with Chain Lane. In later years it was cut through to become the main road and our stretch was reduced to a side road. Another development was the building of Jackson Avenue, leading down to the City Hospital; Chain Lane was widened at the top end into a substantial road connecting to Burton Road, the A38. Our local farmer in my day was named Mellor, whose farmhouse was about 100 yards up the lane towards Keats Avenue. Dad kept his car in one of the farm sheds.

The golf links made a handy playing field and adventure area for Nev and me, especially if our friends Esme Welch and Dorothy Round came with us, though mostly we played 'tough' games like climbing trees and Cowboys and Indians; we didn't bother much with girls at that age. Esme's father was the manager of Derby's most important clock shop, renowned Smith of Derby (they installed the first cathedral clock in St Paul's). Another near neighbour was Alan Ainsworth in a detached house about four doors away. His folks must have been very well off because local kids were sometimes treated to a movie session in their garage, when his Dad showed black-and-white novelties like Felix the Cat and Mickey Mouse. This would have been in 1932 or so when I was seven; Felix was my favourite.

Just inside our end of the golf links down Keats Avenue a tiny stream, hardly bigger than a wet ditch, offered ample supplies of fresh watercress for the house. Also we lads would venture out onto the nearest fairways and help the golfers look for lost balls – by kicking them under a tussock of grass and standing on them until the golfers had gone by: boys will be boys! My usual practice was to take home the best finds, wash them thoroughly, and then sell them for sixpence each to Uncle Horace whenever he came over on a visit.

Mom and Dad were not active churchgoers, but they had a good work ethic and were frugal and sober. Beyond mere survival, their main aim in life was to ensure that their two sons had the best education that they were capable of achieving. Dad in particular, a skilled artisan, was aware but not ashamed of his own academic shortcomings, and he had the good sense to nurture the potential of his boys. As to the church and my childhood, I was usually taken to Sunday school in Littleover by Miss Hilda College who lived a few doors away, involving a walk of about a mile and a half each way. I did not enjoy it and gave it up as soon as I was no longer pressed.

To put things into perspective, if we think of the year 1930 when I was five, we had barely settled in at number 53; the end of the Great War was 12 years behind us and the Second World War was looming up nine years ahead. Only 21 years between the end of one world war and the start of the next! I was too young to appreciate our good fortune that Dad had a job, an income and a car, old wreck as it was, which he needed for his work. He worked from eight till six every day, plus Saturday mornings till 1.00 pm. At home he also used all available daylight hours to grow vegetables in our long back garden. Not satisfied with that, in 1937 he bought a small plot of land behind what became the junction of Chain Lane with Jackson Avenue, to use as an allotment. Tom and I did a lot of digging and double digging under Dad's guidance in garden and allotment. We grew potatoes, greens and root crops of all kinds; there were also many soft fruit bushes like blackcurrants, raspberries, redcurrants and gooseberries. Mum, as usual, was the dutiful housewife: shopping, cooking, washing and cleaning around the clock, seven days a week. She was a clever seamstress, using her treadle operated Singer sewing machine. I learned that as a young girl at home in Birmingham she had helped her mother make cardboard boxes in a version of cottage industry.

With his artisan training, Dad was an expert in what we would nowadays call DIY. He could turn his hand to anything and his nature was too stubborn to let any job beat him. In the evenings, he would sit in his leatherette armchair close to 'his' side of the fireplace in the living room, mending the family shoes and boots. He had several sizes of last and a cobbler's post which he gripped between his knees to support the chosen last. He cut up sheets of leather, stripped off worn soles with pliers and nailed on the new, holding a dozen brass shoe nails in his lips as he hammered away with gusto. For the heavier shoes he stitched on through-soles or half-soles, even taking DIY to the limit by twisting and waxing his own thread for the purpose. Much of the time he had a cigarette drooping down from the side of his mouth, spilling ash down his waistcoat and onto the carpet, much to Mum's disgust. He wore round gold-rimmed spectacles with soft wire end loops to curl round his ears; he wore flannelette collarless shirts with separate starched collars, morning, noon and night, and black boots, laced up with four lace holes and four hook fasteners. He also wore long flannel combs which he tucked under his heels when he put on his boots.

Dad had other hobbies; in his younger days he had been a keen amateur athlete, particularly in cross-country events, as a member of Lozells Harriers in Birmingham. His nickname was Bunnie, or Bun, presumably because all that the other runners saw was the rear end of this little fellow scuttling off into the distance! My brother Tom used to keep the newspaper cuttings which recorded some of Dad's best wins. Dad had been a Lozell's vice-president, as had Mum's father Grandad Deakin before him. By the time we lived in Derby, Dad was no longer a competitor, but he continued to take an active part in the sport as judge, timekeeper and race official for the Amateur Athletics Association. My brother Tom also took up cross-country, being a member of the Derby & County Athletic Club, based at the Wagon & Horses pub on Ashbourne Road at the bottom of Windmill Hill Lane. He tried his best, but he was too sturdy to be fleet of foot. Dad secured many autographs in my album of athletes, including Olympic sprint champion Harold Abrahams and world mile record holder Sydney Wooderson. (In Aden, 1958 we gave a lift in our car to Roger Bannister, the first four-minute miler, and I failed to get his autograph.) Just before WWI, I saw Wooderson easily win a demonstration mile race at the Municipal sports ground in Derby. He trotted round in about 4 min 15 sec, slow in comparison with his world record of 4 min 6.4 sec in 1937.

Uncle Tom had also been an athlete in his youth, a sprinter of some repute. He had served in the Great War as an officer's batman. He would regale any company, including a small boy, with gruesome tales of hardship in the mud of the Somme trenches, but it all seemed so very long ago to my young mind. Perspective is difficult for a young one to grasp. In Derby he worked as a storeman at the Celanese works, makers of artificial silk and similar fabrics. His connections proved useful in later years, as he was able to provide lengths of fabric not normally available in the shops. In his younger days before leaving Birmingham he had been a skilled silver spinner for a company making silver cups and goblets of all kinds. A disk of sheet silver is spun on a lathe and worked by pressing a wooden dolly onto the spinning metal so as to produce a bowl shape. I have a 4-inch bon-bon bowl made by Uncle Tom, hallmarked 1920 which was passed on to me by Elsie when Tom died.

Dad kept canaries. At number 53 he built a shed down the garden where he installed his own cages. Naturally he made these himself from punched wire strips and rods, which he painstakingly soldered together in the sitting room, heating his club-type soldering iron in the bed of the coal fire. He exhibited his birds at local shows, the only one I recall being near Burton. He must have given up his canaries in the late thirties, as we did not take them with us to our next house.

It was not long after we had moved to Chain Lane in 1929 that I started 'real' school in Gerard Street, behind Abbey Street. This was a Victorian building for infants and juniors. I travelled to school on the 'Blue Bus' which groaned and grated its way up Chain Lane, down Burton Road and then Abbey Street. However good I was at school, it was never good enough for my Dad. If I scored 97% at mental arithmetic, there was always George Rumbold who would score 98; and if I scored 98, Rumbold would get 99. Dad wanted to know where I had gone wrong and cautioned me to pay attention! In doing this he was not angry or critical, merely giving expression to that heartfelt desire for his boy to do well. When I left school in 1936 the headmaster wrote in that same autograph album – which I still have – "Ever your friend, F. Lockyear".

In my childhood days the working man's annual holiday was just one week and, as we lived virtually in the centre of the England land mass, we could only go to the seaside once a year. We went twice to Llandudno, where I recall the beautiful Conway Bridge and our crossing the Menai Straits to the island of Anglesey. Llandudno had the attraction of a vast flat sandy bay, which had to be patrolled by guards on horseback because of the hidden danger when the tide came flashing in. On top of the western Great Orme headland was a fascinating camera obscura from which one could spy on the whole beach spread out on the circular viewing table under the large prism in the dome overhead – magic!

Our more frequent annual holidays were to Bournemouth or Torquay. These always involved Saturday to Saturday full board in a so-called boarding house – organized by letter in good time ahead by Mother, who could send off an enquiry and get a reply on the next day but one. For the Bournemouth run we would leave Derby early on Saturday morning, driving first to Dolly's house in Handsworth, Birmingham. Then we would set off via Kenilworth, Banbury, Oxford, Andover and so on through the New Forest via Lyndhurst. Route planning meant following signposts from town to town, not by road numbers.

Horace had a superior sort of car and he was a sporty type of driver who probably managed as much as 55 mph on the open road. All the main roads went directly through the centre of the towns and here he would be more circumspect about his speed. Dad, on the other hand, would plod along steadily at 45mph, with the difference that he did not reduce speed in towns if he could help it. Things usually balanced out quite nicely by the time we stopped for a picnic in the New Forest.

The journey to Torquay was more ambitious. After Newbury, the route took us over Salisbury Plain, past Stonehenge and on via Exeter; it was a total of 240 miles from Derby, but by starting out at four in the morning Dad made it in eight hours, including stops, to arrive in time for an afternoon visit to the beach. An average speed of 30, but rarely reaching 50, was a terrific achievement, especially as he drove single-handed, though things could be a bit fraught if a traffic jam built up on the dreaded new Exeter by-pass, which did more harm than good when it was first built, as I remember.

My main seaside activity was to sit and play on the sands, build sand castles and paddle. I had not yet learned to swim; Tom couldn't swim and neither could Dad. On one occasion we were on the beach at Poole harbour near Bournemouth when Tom and I joined an unauthorized trip with some lad in a dinghy which drifted away from the shore. Panic levels increased and the boat started rocking when I foolishly stood up, Dad now shouting instructions from the beach. Luckily the water was very calm and Dad solved matters by wading out to save us – water up to his chin when he reached the boat. Someone else must have paddled us ashore. I learned later that in his young days Dad had been a very good if impetuous diver at the baths, even though he couldn't swim. Apparently he would make his dive and then do a desperate dog paddle to the side, only to go back for more. In my day I duly went swimming once a week with my school to the chlorine stinking public baths in Queen Street, but I stayed at the shallow end with one foot on the bottom and one hand holding the side. The standard of teaching could not have been very good. I finally learned to swim in quite different circumstances.

Our other family excursion, sometimes not including Tom as he grew out of his teens, was the traditional family day out in the car. We would drive out into Derbyshire through Belper, Matlock, Leek, Buxton or Ashbourne, or any permutation within that perimeter. Dovedale, Alsop-en-le-Dale and Wirksworth were favourite variants among many; Chatsworth, Haddon Hall and Ladybower reservoir were others. Mother usually took a picnic in the form of all the raw ingredients and when we stopped she cut up a loaf of bread on her lap, buttering the exposed end of the loaf before each slice was cut. The same routine was followed for those long holiday journeys, though the fillings were then more ambitious. The Co-Op loaf would be full size, white, soft and fluffy, sold on our street from a horse-pulled van. I do not recall ever seeing sliced bread. Brown bread may have existed, but I never saw any.

Dad's job at Avery's took him all over Derbyshire, not only to collect and deliver scales from shops and coal merchants, but also to repair weighbridges installed at limestone quarries or in town squares. Coal lorries had their sack scales at the back of the wagon, revealed when the tail-board was dropped. If I was not at school, I would get the chance to go with him on such trips, so I got to cover the county between Derby and Buxton pretty thoroughly. Even the very largest weighbridges capable of taking a loaded lorry are supported by beams on a set of small knife-edges on which levers under the platform are hung. When a repair is carried out, the weighbridge has to be tested in the presence of an inspector from the Weights & Measures Department by stacking 56-lb weights first in one corner, then another and so on. Dad may have been small, but he had big hands and was very strong. He lifted those weights two at a time as he nonchalantly transferred twenty or thirty of them from one corner to another. The knife-edges themselves were refurbished by him back at the workshop in Sadler Gate, each one being filed by hand in the bench vice before being hardened in his open coke furnace with its foot-operated blower. To watch that horizontal file flashing backwards and forwards in the hands of a master craftsman was to see simple harmonic motion in action.

Without doubt the two favourite toys for boys in my day were Meccano and model trains, preferably Hornby. I had a selection of both; Bassett-Lowke beauties were well out of my range. Like so many families, our practice was to live in the back room that served for both living and dining, cluttered with fireside chairs, sideboard, dining table and chairs and in our case even an upright piano. At meal times I sat squashed onto the piano stool with my back to the piano and my elbows on the keyboard lid. One day, at the age of about 15, I turned round and started to play the keys. Mother seized the chance and propped up a book of fingering exercises by Czerny before me. Well, why not? They had been good enough for a young Chopin to practise!

Despite the obstacles of Dad mending shoes and Mum on her sewing machine, I somehow managed to weave my train circuit in tortuous bends around the perimeter of the room, mostly on the lino beyond the edge of the Axminster four-by-three (yards) carpet. The clockwork engine needed a spring-busting full wind to get a train to complete one non-stop circuit. The sideboard and chairs served as my tunnels.

In my case, the Meccano outfit held priority over the train set. I built up quite a kit over a period of years and made many ambitious models, tending to specialize in working mechanisms like cranes, tractors, winches and differential gearboxes. I had a clockwork motor to drive these marvels. My favourite trick was to rig up a ski lift hanging from the picture rail and trailing right across the room, carrying nuts and bolts as cargo in a tip-up bucket. The alternative was a turntable crane which hung out over the edge of the dining table to lift loads from the floor below, providing I put on sufficient counter-balance weights. The front room of the house was furnished with a mock Chinese carpet and three-piece suite in uncut moquette, reserved for visitors and not used more than three times in a year. It was too expensive to contemplate lighting a coal fire to keep another room warm.

With such a low traffic density in those days we kids were able to play marbles in the street, along the gutter. We rolled them with an underhand action, rather than flick them with the thumb as is done at competition level. Indoors, the marbles were rolled along the length of the hallway in whichever house we happened to be playing. Cigarette cards were all the rage too, and as most of our parents smoked there was no shortage of supply. The main game was for one player to prop a card against a wall, then the opponent flicked his card from two yards away to knock down the target. Failed shots were left on the floor where they fell. You took it in turns on a winner takes all basis. A hallway with the door closed at the end made an ideal battle ground, lino floor essential.

A more serious pursuit was to collect the cards in sets, with school playtimes providing a good opportunity to go looking for swaps. Specials like a Jack Hobbs could cost as much as 10 routine cards. Outdoors, one of the 'in' toys was the spinning top, where the idea was to keep your top going as long as possible by lashing it with a whip, a leather thong attached to a stick. Yo-yos came and went in popularity, even the diabolo (a sort of double-ended top) and the bowling hoop. The hoop was a wooden ring the size of a small bicycle wheel and pronounced something like 'bowel'; the general idea was to bowl it along the pavement by hand, or with the help of a small stick, as fast as you could run. The original Edwardian version used a metal hoop on which was hooked a metal rod.

It is easy now to forget or overlook things which we took for granted when we were children. For example, house-to-house deliveries of staple items such as coal, bread, milk and vegetables were all available from horse-drawn carts or vans. Mum not only went out to make her purchases as necessary, she would also nip back with a bucket and spade to shovel up any equine output for use in the garden. The horses used by the roundsmen knew what they were supposed to do – they clopped along a few doors at a time in response to a 'coom-up' from the driver who by then was well down the street. We kids used to hang on to the back of the wagon for a free ride if no-one was looking. On one occasion I fell off the side of the greengrocer's wagon and got dragged underneath the rear wheel, which ran over my left upper arm. Luckily there is plenty of soft flesh there and no bones were broken. On another occasion I was at a bonfire night party when a child swinging a sparkler hit me in the eye with his flame thrower. I was rushed to a local doctor who flushed out any sulphurous foreign bodies and no lasting damage was done.

In the early 1930s, all four of my grandparents lived in Birmingham, as did all branches of the family except us. The Southertons lived in Farm Street, Hockley Brook; the Deakins in Church Street, Lozells. Dolly and Horace lived in Handsworth. All these places are central or suburban districts of Birmingham. By this time, Uncle Tom and his wife Elsie lived in our old house at number 49 Jackson Street; they later took over the Drury Lane corner shop at number 1. The usual pattern was for us to take Tom and Elsie in our car to Gran Deakin's for Christmas. We drove from Derby via Burton and Lichfield, a journey which in the depths of winter was easier said than done. The Burton area around the confluence of the rivers Dove and Trent was notorious for its thick fogs at a time when all households had coal fires, not to mention factories using coal-fired boilers. There was no by-pass then. The route through the middle of Burton took us via the humpback bridge over the railway line past the Pirelli works, on by the gas works with its many gasometers, then rattling over the multitude of brewery level crossings in the centre of town before getting onto the Lichfield road again. The whole journey could take up to two hours, assuming we didn't get a puncture. The only saving grace was a fish and chip shop in Burton by the gasworks where we would stop for cod and a penn'orth with salt and vinegar to eat in the car, straight from the newspaper wrappings.

Talking of punctures, in the days of inner tubes and cross-ply tyres, Dad's hands were so strong he could remove a tyre from the rim without bothering with tyre levers. Then he would apply a patch to the damaged inner tube while it was still on the wheel and reassemble the whole lot in next to no time, all by the side of the road.

Dolly and Horace would come for the day too, making a

large family gathering. Other great uncles, aunts and cousins might look in. Gran's house was a three-storey terrace in a steep little side street. The back room, the centre of life, had a wide cast-iron fireplace with side oven and spits, and there was a scullery at the back. The only toilet was in a brick outhouse down the back yard, where the throne itself was a whitewood box with a cut-out seat. A bundle of torn newspaper squares hung in a strategic position. Christmas was lots of fun for a small boy; the Christmas stocking could be expected to reveal an orange, some chocolate pennies in a bag, a real sixpence from Horace and a small toy or two. Entertainment was home made. Dad would sing an operatic aria in his fine tenor voice, Mum vamping on the piano in E-flat, opening the way for Dad to finish on a crystal clear high B flat, having already touched the top C (his idol was Enrico Caruso). Then Great Uncle Harry would give his rendition of a cheeky little ditty that had the adult company in hysterics, but which we children were not supposed to understand: something about '… with the end of my old cigar!' Then came Auntie Elsie's booming contralto version of a song from 'The Maid of the Mountains', off-key, and Dad would lighten the atmosphere with a demonstration of a quality tap-dance routine.

There was very little drinking, as I remember. It was said that Grandad Deakin liked his beer, but the others did not usually get beyond a sip of sherry; he was a sheet zinc worker in the building trade. While we were at Gran's for Christmas, my family (except for Dad) usually walked a few hundred yards to visit Grandma and Grandad Southerton for about a few minutes, but otherwise we never saw them again until the following year, if then. Their back-street tenement was little better than a hovel. The unspoken story was that Grandad Southerton had ruined our family's life through booze and my father had left home in disgust as a teenager. I learned later that Grandma was no less to blame, as it seems she went the same way, but I am not qualified to pass judgment.

By the time I was about eight years old, in the summer I was allowed to travel on a Blue Bus from Derby to Handsworth for two weeks' holiday at Dolly's house. Mother put me on the bus in the centre of Derby and off I would go. I had to change buses in Burton, where the bus conductor made sure I caught the right connection. Horace then picked me up at Four Oaks and took me to their house. Horace was in the jewellery jobbing trade; he ran a factory (started by his father) where they made screw and clip earrings, chains, brooches and so on for the trade, everything except the jewel itself. I loved to go to the factory in Northampton Street and watch women working the hand-operated fly-presses, stamping out thousands of bits from endless coils of strip metal. Others sat soldering them together. They were paid by the hundred gross or some such piece-work rate; the more items you produced in an hour, the more your pay.

Dolly and Horace's house in Normandy Road was quite posh by our standards, even though it was only a small house in the centre of a terrace of three. It had advanced features in the 1930s which were not commonplace until after the war. For instance, the front and back rooms had been knocked through but could be separated by folding glass-panelled doors. There was also a toilet off the hall under the stairs, with a magical dispenser bottle attached to the downpipe between tank and pan which discharged a shot of San-Izal disinfectant each time the chain was pulled. The kitchen had been extended at the back into the garden in what we might still call the modern fashion; here Dolly had amazing machinery like a top-loading washing machine and a refrigerator, things I never saw in any other house.

Their first child, my cousin John, was born in 1933 at that house, and on those holidays it became my job to look after him any evening when Dolly and Horace went to visit their friends Edith and Jack White, who lived in an adjacent side street. Jack ran a garage in the area. If I had any trouble I could signal by putting a light on in the back bedroom, which they could see from the back of the Whites' house. I expect I signalled for the fun of it more often than not. One novelty for me at Dolly's house was their Pianola; I could put in a paper roll and play 'Poet & Peasant' like a virtuoso!

In 1936 came my move up from Gerard Street to Bemrose, a new grammar school for boys located on Uttoxeter Road, where my brother Tom had been a founder pupil. He had moved to there from Abbey Street in 1930 when Bemrose was built. In 1933 he left school to become an apprentice with the telecoms branch of the Post Office (later British Telecom) while studying for a degree in electrical engineering as an external student. As I had a preference myself for the maths and science disciplines I must have picked up quite a lot from looking at his study work and the college papers. Tom progressed through the ranks to become head of all GPO factories. During the war, he helped to install secret radar units in many parts of Britain. He retired at 62 (in 1979) as a senior director of BT.

As I grew older and our age gap narrowed, so to speak, Tom and I got a lot of mutual benefit and fun from tackling tricky puzzles in mathematics and geometry. Tom also taught me to play chess, darts, dominoes, solo, cribbage, table tennis and other essential boyhood skills except smoking and snogging. At school I was getting into architecture, from Egyptian and Greek in the classroom to Saxon and Norman by field studies at churches like Repton in the flood plain of the Trent near Burton. Tom was a meticulous sort of artist, who at one time had been on the verge of being articled to a firm of architects. In my final school year I was offered a place at Nottingham University to take an art degree, but the war put paid to that. The war had already taken away my chance to apply for the annual school trip to faraway places in 1940, which in that year would have been Norway. I've never forgiven Hitler for that.

Initially Nev Potter and I walked to school via Corden Avenue, later using Jackson Avenue when it was built. It came out onto the Uttoxeter Road by the City Hospital. We also had the trolley bus, Derby being pioneers in the use of the trolley bus to replace the tram. The trams had previously run as far as City Hospital, but now the new trolley buses came further out to a turning circle opposite the end of Corden Avenue. The Queensway and Kingsway sections of the ring road did not then exist. At the school end of the journey we could have got off opposite the school, but it was better to carry on for one more stop to the Rowditch, not far from the Practising School of my earlier days, where a little sweet shop sold our favourites like sherbet bags and liquorice root to chew.

At Bemrose, discipline was strict and study was a serious

business, but we had all the benefits of such modern facilities as playing fields, gymnasium, science lab, woodwork shop, library and refectory. Football, cricket and athletics were all encouraged and I rushed into these with more gusto than success at the top, only managing an occasional outing with any first eleven. On the other hand I was pretty fair at gymnastics and had a regular place in the display team. The school motto was *Non fallunt futura merentem* which roughly translates as: *The future does not fail the deserving*. The school had been designed to hold 400 pupils, but it grew until during the war years we had over 800, including at times Basque and Norwegian refugees. We were about 40 to 45 in a class and the standard procedure was to move from room to room for each subject.

In the spring of 1937 we were joined at Bemrose by Gordon Stych – as he was then – later changed by Deed Poll to Styche. Before long, a gang of five had been formed, namely Nev, Gordon and myself, Tony Wall and Don Record. By our teens Don was 5ft 11in tall, Tony 6ft, Gordon 6ft 4in and Nev over 6ft 5in. I was the short one at barely 5 ft 9 in. After those school days, Don went on to become a county land surveyor, Tony a director of Qualcast of lawn mower fame, Gordon a turbine blade foundry manager at Rolls Royce aero engines and Nev a Lloyds Bank branch manager. I joined the army, perhaps not then realizing there was a lot more to come.

Gordon was a fine bat and fearsome fast bowler who virtually carried the First XI on more than one occasion. Nev Potter was a good left arm spin bowler, dropping them down from a great height, but he was at his best on the football field. He played left wing, although a natural right-footer. This incredibly tall lad would lollop down the left wing at his unhurried pace. He was too big for schoolboy opponents to tackle him in any direct fashion, but they would dance around his legs while he allowed himself to be drawn deep into the left corner. Then he would turn to face the wrong way back up the line and defenders would prepare to block any sudden swivel indicating a left-footed centre, leaving Nev to put in his unexpected right cross. Waiting in the centre would be the diminutive Arthur Osborne, our own clone of Stanley Matthews, or better still Tommy Powell, who kicked like a cannon shot. No schoolboy goalkeeper could hope to stop one of his shells. He went on to captain the all-England youth team, eventually playing for the Rams of Derby County.

By now I had progressed to a bicycle, having had my one and only lesson from Auntie Elsie. She had man-handled me and the bike down Keats Avenue, gripping the saddle and pushing at ever increasing speed until "Goo on, pedal the bluddy thing!" So I did, straight out the end of the avenue, across Chain Lane and into the ditch on the other side. Before long, Nev and I rode our bikes to school, tatty brake cables permitting. A bicycle provided me with good basic mechanical experience, as there were always bearings to dismantle and tighten, brake pads to change, broken chains to mend and wheel spokes to stretch to singing pitch, not to mention the usual punctures. At one stage I had a bike with a back-pedal brake, where one literally cranked a quarter turn backwards to operate a multi-disc brake built into the rear hub. Of course you couldn't have a Sturmey-Archer three-speed gear if you had a hub like that, and expensive Derailleur gears were rare.

When war was declared on 3 September 1939 I was not far off 15 years old, which made me quite 'senior' in the hierarchy of schoolchildren. Preparations against the threat of war had been made for some months, including evacuation plans. These meant that children were to be transferred from the centres of industrial cities such as Derby to supposedly safer rural areas. As soon as war was declared these plans were put into operation, so we older boys had to supervise younger children at collection points for bus and train journeys into the great unknown. "Don't forget your gas masks!" I stayed on in Derby, but coincidentally the family was about to move to a new house, which Mum and Dad were buying; they were very anxious to buy through a mortgage, rather than rent as in the past.

We moved a few days after the war started to number 23 Fairway Crescent, a new development at the edge of another golf links, this one off Kedleston Road behind the junction with Allestree Lane and still on the fringe of Derby. This was the first time Mum and Dad had bought a house, so I can now appreciate it must have been an emotional landmark in their lives. Our back garden hedge was right by the sixth green and

I soon learned how to nip over the hedge with a mashie-niblick left with us by Uncle Horace and a putter for four holes of pitch and putt for free.

I now had a journey of about three miles to school, so the bicycle became all-important; so too were the yellow oilskin leggings and cape for foul weather travel. These essentials were rolled up in a leather belt fastened to the back of the saddle when not in use. My route took me via Kedleston Road and Queensway, which was part of Derby's modern ring road, to Uttoxeter Road. A variation was to go further in towards town, then cut through to Ashbourne Road and so to the Rowditch. That route had the advantage of taking me past the posh Parkfield Cedars girls' school; hockey practice meant acres of underwear for a rude boy to ogle! Before long, school meals were introduced, which was a good thing as there was no hope of getting home in the lunch break. Dad left for work before eight o'clock in the morning, so I couldn't get a lift with him. It meant either bicycle or walk.

Number 23 was a conventional semi-detached three-bedroom house with a half-round front bay window downstairs. The back room had French doors opening onto a small flagged area leading to the lawn, quite a good sun trap where in the autumn Dad would spread out his green walnuts on newspaper to ripen in the sun. Once they were black they would be pickled in spiced vinegar. I still love pickled walnuts. There was a side driveway wide enough for a car and Dad lost no time in building a timber garage level with the back of the house. He bought the raw 4x2 stock and literally cut and jointed it himself in the driveway, aided by Tom (now aged 22) and me when needed. The garage stood on a concrete base and was covered in boards and roofing felt, and there were back and side windows. (I recently discovered it stands to this day.) In the first full year Dad also built himself a greenhouse at the bottom of the garden, again from raw materials. It was used for target practice by the golfers.

All these things took time, but the first serious project when we arrived at number 23 was the need to dig the air-raid shelter. This Dad chose to do at the very bottom of the garden, just before the hedge. It was about 6x4 ft in plan and 4ft high inside. It was made of concrete using whatever reinforcement we could get hold of: iron bedstead frames were favoured. It protruded about a foot above the ground and there were little concrete steps down into this dungeon which turned a corner as anti-blast protection. Our neighbours at number 21, Miss Phyllis Jones and her aged mother, shared our shelter. Phyllis was a Joyce Grenfell sort of character who later became an English teacher at my grammar school, a rare appointment in those days. Other people built something similar or they were issued with an 'Anderson' shelter, a set of curved corrugated iron sheets which were used to span your own pit which you then covered with a thick layer of earth. Another type of shelter was the 'Morrison' made of steel girders, which you built into the house wherever space could be found, sometimes simply as a crawl space under the dining table. It offered protection from falling masonry.

When the first air-raid warnings were sounded we were all very frightened and would dash to the air-raid shelter as fast as we could, taking coats and blankets with us to keep warm, thermos flasks for hot drinks and torch and candles for lighting. Behind the hedge at the bottom of our garden was that small brook, not a foot wide, so before long our shelter became a few inches deep in water and not very hospitable; Dad had overlooked the penetrating power of groundwater when siting our air-raid shelter. People in general tended to get rather blasé after a while and air-raid warnings were often ignored. However, there was one occasion when I was in the kitchen at night after the alarm had sounded and I heard the whistling scream of bombs coming down alarmingly close. As I flung myself to the floor there was a huge bang which seemed to be right inside the kitchen, but no bombs fell on us. They had in fact dropped about 200 yards away. The next morning I found out what our noise was: the front flap of mother's electric cooker must have been in the open position and I had smashed it off with my elbow like a karate chop without feeling a thing! We also learned that more of those 25 lb scatter bombs had dropped on Dad's allotment area and in so doing had blown the tops off his entire potato crop, clean as a whistle. He was not amused.

I lived in that house for only six years until I joined the

Army in 1945 at the age of 20, but of course those had been formative years during which I grew through puberty to young man, soaking up education and worldly wisdom at a high rate. Within that period I completed my schooling, matriculation and higher school certificate, with the emphasis on maths, science, art, English grammar, French and Latin. I served in the Air Training Corps (ATC), including working on aircraft frames, flying formation from Burnaston airfield outside Derby in the Miles Magister trainer. I did my final school year at Bemrose as school captain, 18 months as an Engineering Cadet at Derby technical college (now a university), and passed a War Office selection board – and fell in love!

Burnaston (now home to a Toyota car factory) was on our usual cycling tour around the network of villages such as Findern, Willington and Repton off the A38 Burton Road. I recall visiting an air show there with the family in perhaps 1938 when I was an impressionable young teenager. Among the treats on show was a rare autogyro, this being a sort of helicopter where the blades are not power driven but rotate freely in order to give lift in place of fixed wings. A conventional propeller arranged as a pusher gives forward motion. The slow speed manoeuvrability is excellent. Another special item was a demonstration of aerobatics by renowned RAF pilot Ranald Porteus in a small monoplane. Normally one would expect any aircraft to come in to land against the prevailing wind direction to take advantage of the available runway. Not so, if you know what you are doing! Porteus came in *downwind* just above the runway surface until at the last moment he made a sudden turn to face up-wind, thus deliberately causing the plane to stall, and promptly set it down on the spot. That skilled manoeuvre appealed to my technical mind. Burnaston was a grass field, no concrete runways.

My teenage years were overshadowed by the war. From the age of 16 onwards we boys took turns at fire-watching duty at the school, which meant spending the night touring around all the building including the roof, looking out for any fires on or around the premises caused by incendiary bombs. We slept on camp beds on the stage of the assembly hall. Derby was a prime target for German bombers, being the home of Rolls-Royce, the large railway workshops and many heavy industries. The raiders came over from Germany across the North Sea into the mouth of the Humber and then followed the River Trent for ease of navigation. These were isolated opportunist raids, not to be compared with the saturation attacks such as those on Coventry and other cities. Even so, lives were lost and the constant level of fear was disturbing to morale. People got used to engine noises in the sky, trying to distinguish a Junkers from a Heinkel, or 'that sounds like one of ours'. Searchlights would criss-cross the sky and filthy smoke screens would belch up from the oil drums around the city by-pass.

Bemrose had very large playing fields with football pitches, cricket pitch and athletics track; strangely enough, no space was allotted indoors for sports or games that might have included darts, billiards and table tennis. Older boys played table tennis on a couple of large reading tables in the library but there was no room to leap about at the ends. By then I was school captain and the day came when I pestered for an interview with the education committee in town to submit my plan for them to provide the school with proper tables and nets. This campaign was successful and we were able to use the school refectory to play in earnest. Being head boy or school captain was not really as grand as it sounds, as he was the one landed with the obligatory speech of thanks whenever a dignitary visited. The one I recall was Dame Myra Hess, who gave a piano recital in 1942; Bach's *Jesu, Joy of Man's Desiring* was her speciality. Afterwards the headmaster pushed me forward without a word of warning. I have a copy of her arrangement of that masterpiece among my sheet music.

Soon after my 16th birthday I had joined the newly formed ATC Squadron at school and really took to the training, including Morse code, aircraft recognition, Great Circle and astral navigation and much more. I became a flight sergeant and was one of a few to go for five days to Regent's Park in London for special extra training with aural and sight tests – talk about spots before your eyes! While we were there we went to the Turkish baths and swimming pool in Baker Street, where I learned to swim. My pals taught me how to roll-dive slowly into the water from the edge of the pool, which gave me confidence and I was hooked. One would have thought after all this I would go into the RAF, but it was not to be.

During the summer holidays of 1941 older schoolboys were needed to help farmers during early harvests. About 20 of us went to spend two weeks in Scopwick, a village in the sticks south of Lincoln, where we were billeted in the traditional timber-built village hall. Home comforts involved sleeping on uncomfortable, dusty straw palliasses, which are nothing better than hessian bags stuffed with straw, laid out on the boarded floor. Our daily work that year was to help a local farmer with jobs such as gathering and stacking his fields of black beans, the filthiest crop one could ever imagine. Lincolnshire was well known for its abundance of RAF aerodromes for bomber squadrons and pilot training. We were near to one such training airfield from where light aircraft flew, towing a target drone on a long cable. This plane would go out over the North Sea to provide target practice for trainee fighter pilots. Watching these routine flights, we soon learned that on return to base they would make one pass at low level over the airfield to drop their cable before circling again to land without the tail-end encumbrance. One day the pilot could not disengage his cable so he went round again for another try. His best line was now directly over our heads in the fields, with that cable cracking behind him like a 100-yard whip. We all dived to the ground as he made his approach.

During the war many school children were evacuated from potential German target zones to supposedly less dangerous areas. In addition to this general policy, other families – if they could afford it – set up a second home somewhere out in the countryside so that the family might be safe while the breadwinner commuted as and when. One such family were Horace and Dolly with their three children John, Peter and Anne. They took a cottage in Whatcote (a village not three miles from Upper Tysoe where our own family now live in the green fields of Warwickshire). In 1942 Gordon Styche and I cycled from Derby to Whatcote via Burton, Lichfield, Warwick and Wellesbourne. The plan had been devised by Horace in Sutton Coldfield, Dolly in Whatcote, the farmer, and of course our parents. Off we went, with basic requirements in knapsacks and saddle bags. We navigated by town names rather than by route numbers and took seven hours total. Gordon had a heavy sit-up-and-beg machine, whereas I had a faster touring model with dropped handlebars. We stopped en route for a sandwich, a refreshing slurp of lemonade and to relieve ourselves behind a convenient bush.

Dolly's cottage was down the first lane past the pub and the farm was down the second. We shared a vast bed in an end room which had a primitive bathroom leading off. Our work was anything the farmer needed at the time, mostly pitchforking cut straw on to horse-drawn wagons in the field, then riding back to the farm and building ricks. It was heavy work, but no problem for young lads. Food was provided by the farmer's wife, huge sandwiches and perry cider, eagerly gulped down by those who had no experience of such strong brew. We suffered. And there was a land girl! One day Gordon and I put a spoon of fizzy Andrews salts in her chamber pot; next day she got her own back by folding the sheet to make our bed into a French bed.

Back at home, Dad took on a teenage office girl to handle paperwork, time sheets, small machine sales and such essential routine matters. I was about to start at the technical college and would meet her in passing if I went to the workshop in order to cadge a lift home. When faced with the obligatory National call-up, this girl elected to go in for training as a nurse. She reported to Chesterfield Royal Hospital on the last day of 1943 to begin four long years as a nurse to achieve her fully qualified SRN status. Her starting pay was £3:2/6d per month, buy your own stockings. Whenever she came home to Derby for a day or two my mother would invite her over for tea, so of course I met this young lady in more congenial surroundings. Her name was Betty Richardson, whose family had moved from their native Scarborough in the first year of the war; her younger brother Dennis later attended Bemrose school some four years behind me.

I left school in the spring of 1943 to join an Engineering Cadet course, a wartime scheme set up by the Ministries of Defence and Education. The idea was to produce qualified engineers leading to a commission in a technical branch in any one of the three services (assuming that one achieved the engineering degree and passed the appropriate selection board). I chose the Army and got through. My course base was Derby Technical College, nowadays a new university, so I was able to continue living at home. Subjects included pure and applied maths, theory of structures, theory of machines, engineering drawing and so on, but there was also a range of practical work on machine tools like planers, shapers, grinders, lathes, drills and the like, all collectively known as production engineering. I still have the scribing block test piece I made at the time. Some of the best instructors were Rolls-Royce based. I was entitled to style myself an associate member of the Institution of Mechanical Engineers. After more studies and actual experience, I later upgraded to the top professional level of Chartered Engineer.

Meanwhile my friendship with Betty gradually blossomed into romance, 'gradually' being the operative word because we could only meet when she came home from Chesterfield to Derby. I would sometimes cycle over to her parents' home in Alvaston and I went with her to the railway station when she caught a late train back to work. These were the dark days of war when there were no street lamps which could have given away a town's position to enemy aircraft. Vehicle and cycle headlamps were shielded with slotted metal covers to prevent any upward beam of light. The station was dark and cold at night and kissing and cuddling on the dismal platforms produced many a smudge on my raincoat sleeves. Life was austere for everybody, with the rationing of most foodstuffs, clothing and petrol. Chesterfield lay in a mining area so Betty had plenty of hard work associated with industrial injuries. In addition, more and more wounded soldiers were directed to her hospital, and all this at a time when there few male orderlies because any fit ones had been called up. She certainly earned her stripes. By the summer of 1945 my own course was coming to an end.

ARMY

The more one does, the more clearly are revealed those things yet to be done – as others will be only too quick to point out.

When my call-up papers arrived, complete with a single rail ticket from Derby to Durham, I reported to Brancepeth Castle, a military barracks outside the city. I was now in the army in the General Service Corps, effective 6th September 1945. So began my first six weeks of primary training mainly aimed at fitness, discipline and familiarization with basic weapons. Conditions were basic. Pay was 3/- per day. Along with the serge battledress uniform were items called 'drawers cellular, soldiers for the use of.' In other words, underpants. We did ten-mile route marches in full kit through all the country lanes. For long-range rifle practice, meaning 400 yards and over, we were taken to the ranges on the low-tide foreshore at Sunderland, firing in the direction of the open sea where target boards were erected. After Durham, I went for a short while to a holding depot near Nottingham before being posted to an officer cadet training centre at Meopham in Kent. My pay rose to 5/- per day and I wore a white disk behind the cap badge, denoting this improved status. My 21st birthday came and went unmarked while I was there. The most physical part of this period was the field work that required us to climb a local escarpment carrying weapons and ammunition boxes. We all became very fit, lean and hungry.

My next move at this level was to the Mons Barracks in Aldershot where we came under the guidance of legendary RSM Brittain, Coldstream Guards, reputed to have the most powerful voice in the British army. His high tenor voice would ring out if he saw you at the far side of the enormous parade ground: 'Cadet Smith, walk properly, you're idle … Sah!' His *can belto* would have outgunned Pavarotti's *bel canto*! Even though we were not commissioned he always referred to his cadets as 'Sah'. Classroom training concentrated now on military law, tactics, wireless communications, map reading and logistics; field training included a five-day trip high into the Snowdonia

National Park above Bangor. We lived rough in deep snow conditions while we chased around in mock battle scenarios. Whenever you stopped, procedure taught that you were to get down into a position concealed from view, with a good field of fire, and face the front. One day, as we lay exhausted up the mountain, some chinless wonder came up and said to the shivering lad next to me: 'What are you doing now, my man?' 'I'm f f facing the f f front, sir' Maybe there was another adjective in there somewhere!

Our marching out parade at Mons before some dignitary marked the end of my life as a private soldier and officer cadet. I was commissioned as a Second Lieutenant in the Royal Electrical & Mechanical Engineers, the REME, on 6th April 1946. This was a short service commission, which I upgraded to a regular commission some two years later after taking yet another selection board. These commissions can now be regarded as rare documents, as they are in the name of King George VI. One of them hangs on the wall of my office.

My first posting was to Arborfield in Berkshire, the home of REME, where training now concentrated on repair procedures, workshop location under battle conditions, tank and truck recovery techniques, driver training etc. Then I went for my first placement to an actual workshop, this one in Burscough near Ormskirk in Lancashire. As this had mostly civilian staff doing mundane repairs, I was about as disinterested in them as they were in me. The one great compensation was that the seaside resort of Southport was not far away, where some of us could go for a day out and a theatre trip. Considering my background in table tennis at school, my greatest thrill when visiting the Southport theatre was to see on stage the Hungarian legend Viktor Barna, then regarded as the greatest table tennis player the world had ever known, famed for his backhand flick.

Wheels within wheels, the sister of one of my former teachers at Bemrose had a house in Southport, so a plan was hatched. Betty came up by train from Chesterfield and stayed for a few nights with this family. I proposed and she accepted on 15th June 1946. The engagement ring was a square diamond and sapphire beauty selected from three or four alternatives provided by Horace, and of course Betty wears that ring to this day (there have been gold chains, other sapphires and a solitaire diamond since then). I was upgraded to the rank of full Lieutenant on 6th September 1946. Back to Arborfield for more Corps training and I was being groomed for my first posting overseas.

The notoriously hard winter of 1946/47 was beginning to bite when in January 1947 I left a holding camp above Otley in Yorkshire headed for Southampton, but my initial destination was a base camp near Thetford in Norfolk. It seemed as though the whole of that area was covered in a sheet of ice. My duty was to escort a company of infantry who were heading for the same ship. They had their own warrant officers in charge so my nominal role was to count numbers and tick boxes. In the middle of January we boarded the Dunera, a purpose-built troopship of no more than 12 000 tons, seemingly a luxury liner to my untrained eye. It was headed for Hong Kong. So began my first long sea voyage via the Bay of Biscay, Gibraltar and Malta to Port Said in Egypt. Despite the reputation of Biscay, our crossing on this occasion was calm. After the previous six months of hard training, the conditions on board bordered on the luxurious and I had the chance to go ashore at both Gib. and Malta for a few hours. In Malta a group of us crossed to a bay called Ghajn Toffieha on the west coast, where we had a swim in the warm Mediterranean after wading through yards of deep seaweed.

We disembarked in Port Said in Egypt, which stands at the mouth of the Suez Canal. Two impressions have stayed with me. The first was an unfamiliar stench which pervaded the air, possibly arising from open sewers; the second was the sight of hundreds of men unloading a coal ship by carrying baskets on their backs up a zig-zag slope away from the docks. I had never seen such labour-intensive work. On reflection I suppose the technique was a snapshot of life in the days of the great pyramids, but in that present day these workers were earning their daily pay and I could respect them for that. From there I went first to a local transit camp, but was soon on a train to Cairo where I was to join my new unit.

That train journey recalls a salutary lesson. On boarding the train and at any local stop on the way, the platform would be crowded with small children shouting 'eggs-i-bread' or something like that. They were literally offering hard-boiled eggs and bread to the soldiers leaning out of the carriage windows. But there was a purpose to their game. Typically a soldier would have two or three fountain pens in his uniform breast pocket. At the very last moment, as the train started off, an older boy would run up to a window with a rolled-up tube of newspaper and deftly flick a pen out of an unsuspecting pocket. 'Too late, soldier! That's another pen lost, soon to be sold to a tourist in the nearest souk for a few piastres. Special price for you, mister!

After a grinding train ride in the oppressive heat, I arrived in Cairo and got to my new unit. This was a specialist outfit called the FVPE (Fighting Vehicles Proving Establishment). A grand title, but in reality it was the Middle East branch of the armoured vehicles development centre based in Chobham, Surrey, where all things new in armoured vehicles were developed and tested. This Cairo unit was about 100 strong, one third admin, one third drivers and one third workshops. The workshops section was commanded by a REME captain and I was to be his replacement. Initially, I was billeted in a modern block of flats in the newly developed Heliopolis district of Cairo on the northern side of the city. The British were in the throes of handing over the stewardship of Egypt to the Egyptians (under King Farouk) and concentrating in the lower Canal Zone, south of Ismailia where the Suez Canal opens up into the Great Bitter Lake, the northernmost of the two lakes.

With little to do, I had time to explore the great city of Cairo and adjust myself to life in the Middle East. There were two great thrills which stand out: one was the Grand Prix motor race on the island of Gezira in the river Nile, only the second such event to be held after the war. A few of us went to watch the race from the trackside among the palms. The race was unusual in that all cars were identical little Italian Cisitalia 1.5-litre jobs. The winner was the brilliant Alberto Ascari junior, son of a famous father. My other great privilege was to visit the pyramids and the Sphinx at Giza not many miles south west of Cairo. I duly climbed the long passages inside the great pyramid to the royal chambers, and I also gazed in awe at the seriously damaged Sphinx. One day in Cairo, when I was calmly driving my jeep along an empty boulevard, Egyptian police cars and motorcycle outriders ushered me to the side of the road so as to allow a certain King Farouk and his entourage to sweep by; I graciously conceded.

By April 1947 I had been promoted to captain (at the age of 22 years) and was in charge of my new special workshop unit in time for the move to Kabrit on the bank of the Little Bitter Lake south of a Suez Canal station at the conjunction of the two lakes. We lived in ridge tents and hung mosquito nets over our camp beds. Our frequent friendly visitors were the little land crabs which scurried about in great numbers. The lake edge was only 100 yards away and the daytime temperature was quickly rising to over 100F. We wore khaki drill shorts, shirts, boots and gaiters. It was easy to wander down to the water's edge and swim in the Little Lake. There was also a good open beach on the north side of the point, in other words in the Great Lake, where we could go for some talent spotting.

The local Forces Broadcasting Station studio was also located in that area, known as Kabrit Point. One evening, after shutdown, the anchor man kept the station alive while I sat at the studio piano and played a simplified opening movement of Liszt's Liebestraum over the airwaves; it was not very good, but luckily I was incognito. During another of my escapades I decided to swim alone back to our camp from the Great Lake, the whole way round the point, past the canal station and out into the shipping lane for a few hundred yards, before swinging round westwards again towards our home beach, a distance of about two miles. Very foolish, I suppose.

Apart from keeping our wheeled and tracked vehicles fit for use, the job of my workshop was to manufacture all the experimental bits involved in carrying out trials under desert conditions. One crazy idea was a vertical deflector bar for the front end of a motor cycle, intended to protect a dispatch rider from any booby trap wire across a track. This clumsy device was dangerous in itself; the rider may have been saved from decapitation, but there would be a catastrophic crash. Our most important work started with the arrival from the UK of a secret tank, namely the new 52-ton Centurion. It was good at crossing soft sand, but we experimented with track width extenders to enlarge the contact area and reduce the ground pressure. We made these in my workshop. (By the time I was in Korea 1950/51 we found that the Centurion on its standard tracks was better than American and Russian tanks at traversing deep paddy.)

Another project tackled the problem of winching out a heavy tank stuck in deep sand, in which situation the conventional wisdom is that ground anchors are needed so that cables and winches can be attached. But how do you establish a ground anchor in deep soft sand? We experimented with our own version of a ship's anchor, like a plough blade on a long cable, but in practice this pulled itself deeper and deeper until it travelled underground at what you might call below sea-bed level, because the sand was so deep there was no solid ground to be found. A tank stuck in deep sand needs at least two more like tanks to pull it out again. In extreme cases the tracks may have to be broken so as to reduce rolling resistance, but then there is the catch that no braking is available.

Our unit had custody of three 72-ft, twin-diesel harbour launches in various states of disrepair. One could be cannibalized for spare parts, one was just about seaworthy and only the third was fit for service. The idea was that smaller research projects could be carried out across the Suez Canal on the shores of the Sinai Desert if needed, but for fun we preferred to use the good boat for chariot riding, where a large board such as a wooden door would be towed along at speed, the rider holding a rope as reins. Modern exponents of water skiing don't know what they are missing!

Later a more sinister use for our good boat was called for. We were asked to prepare her for a clandestine reconnaissance trip up the Suez Canal to Port Said, out into the Mediterranean and then eastwards along the coasts of Egypt and Palestine as far north as Haifa. We provided the boat, a mechanic and an officer from our unit. Higher authorities found a Navy lieutenant as skipper and a Royal Engineer officer to carry out secret coastline surveys from the deck. We changed crews in Haifa by driving across the barren Sinai coast road all the way: good fun and a navigational challenge. On my turn at the road trip, as we were driving along the featureless scrub, we saw up ahead what looked like a black carpet laid across the track. We stopped and approached carefully on foot. On closer inspection this proved to be a six-foot wide convoy of multiple zillions of black ants going about their business, another wonder of the world.

Later in the year Chobham was closing down its overseas outposts, so I was posted to join the Royal Artillery of 1st Infantry Division based in Palestine where British troops were in a no-win situation trying to keep the warring Arabs and Jews apart as the establishment of a Jewish homeland was gathering momentum. This I did by travelling yet again via the Sinai coast road, having crossed the Suez at Ismailia, ending up initially at Sarafand, a British base camp near the area now roughly equating to the Gaza strip.

I had now become responsible for the maintenance of the Royal Artillery vehicles and artillery pieces, but my most technical duty was to examine the barrels of the large-bore weapons to approve them as safe for firing, from the 25-pounder to the 4.5- and 5.5-inch field guns. One established method was to push an angled mirror fixed to control rods along the barrel while watching through binoculars as the mirror was rotated, noting the length scale on the rods for accurate location. Next we would send through a pair of pads coated in gutta percha raw rubber to a suspect location; the pads would be cranked open to take an impression of the barrel at that point, so giving precise information on the condition of the barrel.

In this job I travelled around (though not as a tourist) what is now Israel, including Jerusalem and Haifa, and also Jaffa, twin town of Tel Aviv and home of the orange orchards. In early 1948, I got a message that Betty had gone into hospital with a burst appendix and was in a critical condition. I even talked to my father by telephone from a tin hut somewhere in Palestine, a rare feat of communication in those days. The upshot was that I was granted leave on compassionate grounds and sailed on the Empress of Australia from Haifa via Port Said, taking 10 days (sea travel, no flights then). Betty recovered, but I returned this time to Tripoli in North Africa where the 1st Division was by now relocated. Another 10 days in a troopship. Betty and I had talked of marriage, but those laparotomy operations and her general health made that inadvisable. She was off work for six months.

Tripoli, capital of Libya, was under British administration after the end of the war. Libya had formerly been an Italian colony and their influence on the old Arab town was obvious, but the harbour was full of sunken ships. The eastern half of the city had a modern facade and promenade, the Lungomare (meaning alongside the sea), behind which was a myriad of small streets and shops in the European style. The original western end of the city retained its Arab character with alleyways, souks and mosques.

My personal base was in a small workshop unit on the eastern coast but my job of inspecting artillery took me to all the surrounding areas wherever RA gunnery units were camped, from Homs (wonderful Roman ruins of Leptis Magna) in the east to deep in the desert. The ruins of Homs included a rectangular 12-seater marble toilet room with flushing water channels underneath. About 60 miles inland lay the desert town of Garyan, in the foothills. During 1948, a freak storm in those hills resulted in a bore of water rushing down the otherwise dry wadi, only to discharge its main volume of water into our workshop compound to a depth of over 6 feet. Meanwhile our biggest recovery trucks did sterling work out in the hills helping the local population in rescue operations. Near to the city was an old international motor racing circuit, by then taken over by the Americans as a base camp. On the north side was a bay with plenty of sand and good for swimming, sunbathing and socialising.

So there I was, serving on through 1948 and well into 1949, when our earlier plans of marriage were coming into fruition. Betty took the initiative by arranging the day, the church, the banns, clothing coupons and petrol coupons, bridesmaids, reception, honeymoon, and I dare say a lot more. Uncle Horace was to lend us a car. All I had to do was to get home, which I did by securing a seat on the first post-war flight for service people from Tripoli to the UK, on a twin-engined propeller job taking only about 30 passengers. It was noisy, slow and bumpy in the air. I arrived in Derby late on Monday 25th July 1949 and we were married two days later. After a honeymoon at the famous Feathers Hotel in Ludlow, Shropshire, and about two more weeks idling around, we flew back to Tripoli, stopping for refuelling at Nice on the French Riviera. Dear Betty had been plunged into marriage, flying, Army life and the heat of the Middle East in one fell swoop – not to mention unfamiliar shops and Arab souks. She took to it well.

When we first got back to Tripoli as a married couple we were accommodated in the Uaddan, a British Army officers' club which had formerly been Mussolini's casino. Our huge bedroom and bathroom suite featured marble everywhere. Before long we found a small flat on the fourth floor of an office block just off the main shopping street in the eastern town. Deliveries of small staple items like bread, vegetables and even ice blocks for the "refrigerator" were delivered to the high floors by a basket and rope technique, Betty reaching over from the balcony to pull the ropes. The block we lived in had a square central well and on the high floors it was usual for there to be drying lines for laundry strung across from one side to another, on pulleys to assist retrieval. One day, a pair of Betty's silky pants slipped off the clothes line and wafted gently down to ground level at the back of the Olivetti typewriter shop. They were not seen again, presumably having been seized as a trophy. Our so-called oven was a tin box perched on a paraffin flame ring.

Whenever the Royal Artillery fire their howitzers or guns, it is understandable that they prefer to have a spotter up ahead to report back on the actual range and the accuracy being achieved. (A howitzer fires at more than 45 degrees elevation, say over a hill; a gun fires at a lower angle for longer range.) The spotter can be a man on the ground on a convenient hilltop, or even a spy in the sky in a spotter aircraft. In my day the preferred spotters were small Auster high-wing monoplanes flown by artillery officers with pilots' wings. These young bloods tended to be rather daredevil to put it mildly. I took a frightening short flight with one of them. The Auster was a light observation aircraft based on the American Taylorcraft and made in Thurmaston, a suburb of Leicester. In later years, the chief test pilot for Auster was none other than our friend Ranald Porteus mentioned earlier.

My tour should nominally have been for three years, thus until January 1950, but the clever War Office posted me home at the end of December 1949. This time we were to travel on the next available troopship, not a good choice for Betty who can be seasick on a pier. Another problem was that as an officer under the age of 25 years I was not entitled to claim her travel allowance at an officer's rate, which meant I had to pay her fare both to take her to Tripoli and to get her home again. Can you believe it? I should have read the small print.

My next new posting was to join the 8th King's Royal Irish Hussars as their REME officer attached, they being stationed in Oadby outside Leicester, where I reported in January 1950. The scene was set when I spotted two or three of their officers in hunting pink. Before long my new regiment moved to Tidworth barracks on the edge of Salisbury plain. One of the officers had bought a new Morris Minor, a car which had only been out since the Motor Show of 1948.

Betty and I rented a cottage in the village of Appleshaw near Amesbury, not far from Stonehenge. It was little more than a stucco-covered wooden hut, across the lane from the village green where I later played cricket in regulation cream flannels. This cottage was owned by a certain Brigadier Prior-Palmer, who lived in a large house in the village. In 1953 after we had left they had a daughter Lucinda, who became Lucinda Green, champion equestrian who won the Badminton Horse Trials no less than six times.

My car then was a tiny 1926 Austin 7 with manual windscreen wipers, two-wheel brakes and magneto ignition. The tyres on it looked just like WD motor cycle tyres. The long thin gear lever frequently broke off, only to be welded up by one of my lads time and time again. Meanwhile, I had to change gear by using a pair of pliers to grip the broken stub. Starting was dodgy, so Betty gave me a push start in the village most mornings, nightie and dressing gown flapping about, with me running alongside the driver's door until I could jump in. Little Lucy, as we called her, did us proud, making the return journey to Derby at no more than 40 mph flat out. I had bought her off one of the KRIH officers for £45, as he wanted the money for an engagement ring.

While we were in Tidworth, three other officers and I zoomed off early one morning to Silverstone to watch a 500cc race. One of the young drivers obviously had an underpowered machine, so he fell back on the long straights, but when it came to the corners he cut through the pack like a knife through butter. His name was Stirling Moss. He coasted in to second place when his engine blew up 100 yards short of the line.

The regiment belonged to the 'fire brigade', which meant that in the event of a United Nations emergency we would be the first to go, wherever that might be. We did not have long to wait. The Korean conflict was hotting up, the Chinese army joining in against the American forces in the north. The 21st Infantry Brigade was hurriedly assembled and prepared for a war footing. We were to be the first armoured regiment to be issued with the latest tank in the British army, the Centurion. I went to the Barnbow armaments factory in Leeds to accept these tanks, which had to be sent directly for shipment to Korea. Not even the colonel knew that I had worked on them some three years earlier in the Canal Zone of Egypt.

We sailed from Southampton in October 1950 on the Empire Fowey, while Betty went back to nursing in Chesterfield. We were quickly loaded up with various inoculations and vaccinations, including typhoid fever, yellow fever, blackwater fever and Japanese encephalitis. We arrived in the Korean southern port of Pusan about 30 days later, having gone ashore for a few hours at Colombo on Ceylon, Singapore and Hong Kong on the way. As our route took us through the Suez Canal, I was able to see the site of my old workshop at Kabrit point. An advance party of Hussars had travelled earlier and gone to the north to assess the situation. Our two Hussar lieutenants were killed during that reconnaissance.

Our ship was welcomed in Pusan by an all-black American brass band zooming up and down the quayside at double-quick time. The weather was turning icy cold as we made our way to a camp on the outskirts of Pusan to await the arrival of our wheeled vehicles and tanks on various ships. My workshops equipment was mounted on Bedford 3 ton machinery trucks for total mobility in the field and we had just one Scammell 6x4 (six half-axles, four of them driven) recovery truck with extending jib, hopelessly inadequate for working on a large tank. The jib did not even traverse.

South Korea was a poor agricultural country that had long

suffered under Japanese occupation. The countryside consisted of endless rice paddy fields spread out between rolling hills. The few roads were no better than dirt tracks raised up on embankments or bunds which wound their way through the paddy. They were not up to heavy traffic occasioned by the war, so they had to be maintained by US army engineers who rolled and graded the surface day after day. There were no side defences, just a 6-foot drop into the paddy ditch below on both sides. When we did set off to the north, snow was falling heavily and the temperature dropped like a stone. Where the road wound round the side of a hill by Taegu, revealing a vast chasm on the outer flank, one of my precious workshop trucks slid irresistibly off to the side on the treacherous ice. The driver was one of my experienced sergeants who clambered out fast, rolled underneath his truck and watched it smash its way into the valley below. No one was hurt, but my technical resources had been depleted.

The winter proved to be the worst so far in that century and trying to work on vehicles at minus 40 degrees was dangerous, instantly ripping the skin off the fingers. The standard issue gloves for the British army in Korea consisted of three layers: an inner layer of silk, a layer of wool and finally a layer of cotton camouflage. The two inner layers were held on long tapes which passed up through one sleeve and down the other, so that the gloves could be pulled off without dropping on the ground. Obviously such gloves were not designed for use by vehicle mechanics, who took to wrapping hessian around their hands when working near ice-cold armour plate. Our diesel fuel for the Scammell froze in the drum and had to be thinned with petrol.

In that first winter north of Seoul I suffered a severe breathing allergy, which ended up with my being taken to the nearest American MASH field hospital. That was where I spent Christmas 1950, receiving round the clock high volume jabs of some sort for 72 hours. I could not claim to be critically ill, but I did see casualties arriving by truck or helicopter to receive emergency attention, unfortunately not always successful in front of my eyes. Whirlybirds were like little flying beetles, not the powerful air-sea rescue size we know today. Wherever my workshop was pitched we would see bloodied civilians trudging their way to the nearest medical attention they could find. As I drove through the capital Seoul one day, I had come upon an abandoned scout car, so I checked whether it could be recovered. There was no driver to be seen behind the wheel, just both his lower limbs and feet, still on the pedals.

The battle known as Gloucester Valley is well recorded. Some of our Centurions were in that dreaded valley of death, not in a tank battle as such, but trying to extract our infantry fighting a hopeless battle of numbers against the hordes of Chinese. The 8th Hussar tanks were under the command of Major Henry Huth, our most decorated officer. I was at the exit from the valley in my jeep as his tank rolled out and he told me he had been reduced to firing high explosive shells over open sights at the swarms of advancing Chinese. Such was the sickening level of desperation in the attempt to save the remnants of the Gloucester heroes. Our beloved regimental MO Captain Doug Patchett stayed with the troops and was captured, to become a prisoner of war. Doug and I had adjacent cabins when we sailed on the Fowey. A week later when I went up to the line, I called in at a medical post in a clearing off the rough road and supped a canteen of tea with the new MO, named Beer. Later in the day on my way back I found that the whole site had been destroyed by North Korean artillery shells and the MO had been killed along with many others. The site had been deliberately ranged by the Chinese as they withdrew. I missed that disaster by chance, and here I am in great sorrow to tell you of it.

The UN forces had total air superiority but the Chinese were clever. As they withdrew northwards, they would re-form high up on the northern slope of a convenient hill and dig some tunnels through the hilltop to come out on the south face. Their artillery weapons would then be run out to the mouth of the tunnel on the south side, fired and immediately withdrawn. By the time their firing point had been located, they would have gone back out of site, well protected from our response from land or air.

Up ahead I advanced by creeping along a shallow stream bed in the jeep until I took a swing up a hill in fog. Navigation was by sense of balance on the slope rather than by sight. Our infantry up there handed over a young Chinese soldier as prisoner of war and I took him back to the cages at our nearest base. He appeared to be barely 16 years of age; the Chinese used these lads as cannon fodder. Finally, one morning, our colonel's batman peered out of his bivouac, looked at the filthy weather and said: 'Snowin' again, what a fookin' regiment!' In the summer, where a track came upon a small river, a signpost in the middle of the water said: 'If this sign is submerged, the ford is impassable,' an American engineers' joke.

These were hard times for the Korean people. Our troop movements were mostly in a north-south direction and there were more individual farm houses than villages or towns. The houses were simple square structures, raised above the paddy, with an undercroft which had a fire or furnace in one corner. The smoke stack was on the diagonally opposite corner, the whole scheme thus providing underfloor heating. The inner walls of the houses were made of sheets of paper on timber frames, as were the internal sliding doors. Everyone slept on the floor. Often we would see the man of the house cutting across his patch to spread the animal waste, which he did by ladling it out from a conical pot carried in an A frame on his back. He and other family members would use the same frame to carry large bundles of faggots or sticks. When the ladies were working in the rice paddies, one of them might have a new-born baby wrapped in cloths on her back. At feeding time she would simply slip the baby round to one side and swing a long, pendulous breast under her arm to that side so that the infant could suckle. Then back to work.

In one of the towns we came across a deserted college with much of its equipment still intact. In what must have been the biology lab I saw large chests containing hundreds of specimen bugs, beetles and butterflies, all in good condition and beautifully presented. In another room we found a small one-pedal harmonium in working order, so we 'borrowed' that for the duration. My lads cleaned it up and I played hymns whenever I led a basic field service on a Sunday.

During 1951 I was entitled to one week's leave in Japan, reached by train to Pusan and then a Dakota flight to Kure, a former submarine base on the southernmost island, not far from Hiroshima, site of the first atomic bomb. For the return trip I took a Japanese tramp ship (the Hakodate Maru) where the crew were fiercely playing mah-jong in the smoke-filled bowels of the ship. The Yanks called these trips R & R, meaning rest and recuperation; the British called them 'I & I', inebriation and something else. These military tales are indicative of a much wider story; for over 60 years I have resisted the temptation to speak of such things, but I now feel able to release pent-up emotions without a guilt complex. War is not to be glorified. My wife, family and friends will forgive me.

At the close of 1951 came another 30-day troopship home; we didn't have air travel then. Communication had always been by letter, and I had learned that Betty's brother Dennis, by now a young deck officer in the Merchant Navy, was due to join the crew of a small cargo boat of only a few hundred tons on its way from the Gulf to the UK. Yes, you've guessed it; our two ships arrived in Aden harbour on the same day, a supreme coincidence. He cheekily borrowed his first mate's jacket to boost his status, came aboard my liner to a piped reception and was taken to meet the captain. Then he joined my gang of pals for endless pink gins until the ship sailed, when he suddenly realized he was still on board. In the nick of time he got off with the harbour pilot and safely back to his ship. He arrived back in England about two weeks after me, due to his slow speed and the weather in the Bay of Biscay. A good job too, as he was due to be married on 19th January.

My stormy passage through the Bay at the end of 1951 took three days under the most severe conditions I had ever encountered in five otherwise calm traverses. During the second period of 24 hours we actually achieved a negative mileage. Little did I know of the drama about to unfold as the weather deteriorated. This was the time of the *Flying Enterprise* under the command of Captain Henrik Carlsen, who stayed with his sinking cargo ship until the dramatic end. Young Dennis later sailed through that maelstrom, not many days after I had done so, and the plight of his little ship also hit the national headlines. Happily, I was able to travel to Los Angeles in January 2002 to attend his Golden Wedding celebrations.

Our own ship had called in at Hong Kong to pick up more passengers, so I went ashore for a look around, during which time I bought a length of suiting. On my docking in Liverpool, HM Customs charged me import duty on the cloth! In other words, after serving one whole year at the height of the Korean War, that was my reward. Luckily, I was welcomed ashore in Liverpool by Betty's warm tears; the British media were nowhere to be seen. And no, despite the wartime engineering cadetship and 14 years service I do not get any army pension, but I am not likely to forget Korea: their national flag acts as a dust cover over my laptop to this day.

After Christmas my new posting was to the REME Inspectorate headquarters in Chislehurst, Kent. We found a pleasant semi-detached house to rent in the suburb of Petts Wood. In that village there is a plaque to the memory of one William Willett, who in 1907 had promoted the idea of daylight saving. I was now busy composing technical documents. The 610-bhp Rolls Royce Merlin V-12 engines as used in the Centurion tank were to be reconditioned in a Rover factory. These were basically the same engines as those powering the Spitfire, Hurricane and other aircraft, but without the high altitude superchargers. My job was to compile the standards for the refurbishment or repair of components (technical writing again).

We were in Petts Wood for two years and met some lovely neighbours. We were able to see some of the London theatre attractions, including the Mousetrap in its early days. In that first year we spotted the Golden Arrow as it flashed through our local railway station, and we decided to book a trip for ourselves. This meant going up to London to catch the train, and so off we went to Paris for a week. We stayed in a cheap hotel on the Left Bank and did all the tourist bits, including the Eiffel Tower, the Folies Bergères and the Lido night club. Lots of girls, only one costume!

We have now reached 1954, when I was sent on a course to Bovington near Lulworth Cove in Dorset. The aim of this course was to study the principles of tank design, whereby one learns to balance the conflicting requirements of engine size, armour, weapon size, total weight, vehicle speed, manoeuvrability, and so on. On the practical side, we had the option of driving or gunnery training on the Centurion, so as I had driving experience in Korea I chose the gunnery course; I came away with the rare military qualification of *tt*, meaning Tank Technologist. For that year, Betty and I found a cottage in Swanage, high on the west cliff overlooking the sea.

Another of those on the course was an Australian major named Syd Barber. We helped him to find rooms in the cottage next to ours and became friends with him and his wife Peg. That next-door house was owned by Lady Anna Craven, an eccentric rich widow who kept her family crested solid silver cutlery in a shoe box. She would be inclined to dry wet clothes over an electric radiator, leave the iron on, the stove on; and generally frighten Peg and Syd in the flat above. Syd had served in the Far East with the Anzacs during the War but had been captured by the Japanese in Singapore. He was taken away on a hell-ship to Japan suffering great privation, and his health affected forever. He respected the fact that I had served in Korea. Syd and I took it in turns to drive over the downs from Swanage to Bovington every day, this in the days of myxomatosis. The roadside was littered with hundreds of dead rabbits. The course finished in the autumn and Peg and Syd were due to return to Australia. We gave them a farewell dinner at a hotel in Knightsbridge and finally went on board their ship to see them off until the call came out: "All ashore". But that was not the end of that. In later years we were to visit them in their own home city of Canberra.

This time my move was to a branch of the War Office based in Duncannon Street off Trafalgar Square by the side of South Africa House. We found a flat in North Finchley, just south of Tally Ho corner on the old Great North Road. My daily commute was by tube. For this I dressed as a city gent with umbrella, Homburg and rolled newspaper – not really my scene. The flat was on the first floor of a smart house owned by a Jewish family; they were charming people in the rag trade and quite well off. He owned a long bonnet Rover saloon, but when the carburettor played up he simply bought a new car. I was struggling with an old Hillman Minx. Our flat was partitioned off at the head of the stairs. It had large rooms and a luxury bathroom, with smoked glass mirrors everywhere. On Fridays all their family came home for a traditional meal. The smell of fish was … memorable! During this time I enrolled at the Regent Street Polytechnic in order to improve my academic status, resulting in my elevation to Chartered Engineer, this being the highest possible combination of both the academic and the management aspects of my profession.

My job in the War Office was to analyse fault reports on armoured vehicles coming in from all British Army units, liaise with Chobham for repair procedures and from these compile the authorized maintenance documents for issue in standardized form. Many of them concerned the Centurion tank that I knew so well. This kind of work was just up my street, with its high content of technical writing in a precise form, a good continuation from my work in Chislehurst. There was also the experience of working in central London, with opportunities to explore famous spots like Piccadilly Circus, Trafalgar Square (coffee in the Lyons Corner House), The Strand, Leicester Square, Covent Garden, Whitehall, St Paul's, Bond Street, Fleet Street, Oxford Street, Regent Street, and so on.

In this job I had to have ultimate security clearance, which one day came in very useful: I was chosen to join a team of officers from the three services on a secret mission to Malta, where we were to assess the suitability of certain beaches and their hinterland for the supposed landing of tanks and other heavy equipment in the event of any future large-scale deployment of troops if an emergency arose. It was all to do with water depth, beach slope, ground conditions and inland routes. One perk of that mission was that we were treated to a family lunch with the Governor.

At the end of 1956 I was promoted to major and posted to Aden, then a British colony at the southern tip of Arabia and once a vital oil bunkering and watering stop-over on the commercial shipping routes via the Suez Canal to the Far East. I had called in there on my way to Korea in 1950 and had met Dennis there on my way back at the end of 1951. My new job would be on the staff of the garrison as the senior REME officer responsible for all workshops from Somaliland in the Horn of Africa and round the Arabian coastline to Bahrain. This would be more of a management than a technical role, dealing with staff, supplies and policy.

I flew out in December 1956, but because of the unsettled situation in the Canal Zone a diverted flying route took me via Algiers, Kano in Nigeria, along the line of the Equator to Nairobi and then northwards to Aden. At the Algiers stop, on the edge of the airfield, I got my first look at the new Citroen 2CV, where some local farmer proudly demonstrated how well the independent suspension coped over a rough field. On arrival in Aden I was met by one Captain Peter Towers, REME, who was serving with the Aden Protectorate Levies (APL). I had put my new Major's epaulette sleeves onto my khaki drill uniform during the flight; I was one month short of my 32nd birthday.

Peter's career followed an entirely different pattern from mine; he served for some 28 years. He had started as a boy apprentice engineer but went on through the ranks until being commissioned. At various times he was a champion boxer, champion shot and captain of the REME cricket team. Towards the end of his career he was an instructor at Sandhurst military college with the rank of major. We are close friends to this day.

Betty followed in the January, but her own route was via Malta, Kano and Entebbe in Uganda, later made famous by the Israeli rescue of a hijacked plane. Even the experience of life in Tripoli did not prepare her for the humid heat of Aden, 90 degrees F and 90 per cent relative humidity, night and day the same throughout the year. Perspiration tended to run down your body even if you stood still. Aden is a bit like Gibraltar, being an igneous rock peninsula attached to the mainland by a causeway. The difference is that Aden is barren, having even less foliage than Gib. On the north side of this rocky lump is the main town and harbour called Steamer Point. On the eastern side is another town at a small bay called Crater City, which sits in the hollow of an ancient volcano. In those days the only road connecting the two parts went through a narrow pass; there was no coastal road. The airfield at Khormaksar cuts across the neck of the peninsula, similar to the situation at Gibraltar. The outer reaches of the airfield also double as a camel racing track, a very colourful event embracing all the aspects of a typical UK racecourse. The jockeys are usually very small lightweight boys, but it is a marvel how they get the camels to race in a competitive sense as horses will do. It just does not seem natural.

As a married officer I was entitled to a residence or 'quarter,' but initially the only one that could be found was a private rental flat in Crater City. We soon moved to the western end of Steamer Point bay, on a promontory with wonderful aspects over the harbour and the Indian Ocean. The building allotted to us was just a former canteen hut, reached by a bridge over a dry moat; this was the only 'quarter' I had in my entire army career. The area was the site of an old fortress: some of the huge gun barrels dating from Victorian times still lay around and the communication tunnels were like rabbit warrens beneath us. Not 400 yards away stood the Governor's residence, so when we heard the bugle and saw the flag being lowered at 6.00 pm we knew it was time for our first gin and tonic. Much further round the bay and accessed by a causeway road is an area called Little Aden, the site of the oil storage tanks used for bunkering ships passing through the Suez Canal.

My job as a staff officer gave me great opportunities to visit the whole of the southern coast of the Arabian Peninsula, from Somalia in the Horn of Africa, Aden itself and on to Mukhalla, Salalah, Musqat, Fujairha, Ras-al-Khaima, Trucial Oman, Sharjah, Abu Dhabi and eventually Bahrain. At the airport there I had the privilege of standing by the new secret Vulcan bomber on the ground. I got into conversation with the navigator (naively thinking to brandish my ATC training) and asked him how they navigated from the UK to Bahrain. He replied: 'At the speed of this thing we don't bother about details; we go straight up until we get half way, then we come straight down again!' RAF humour.

While in Sharjah I would also visit nearby Dubai for a day out. In each of these places the local sheikdom would have its own army, usually called Scouts or Levies. If they had a supporting workshop the local fitters were led by a REME sergeant under my staff officer supervision. To make these trips I had to thumb a lift with any RAF flight going my way. These outposts had very basic airstrips and the form was for the pilot to do a noisy low altitude circuit until the duty watch came out of his hut, lit a smoke flare as a wind indicator and gave clearance. Aden itself was a much bigger set-up, having a base workshop as well as the home of the APL. British army troops had a camp in Little Aden. I had to ensure these little workshop units had REME leaders with the necessary level of experience, involving lengthy negotiations with Middle East command in Cyprus by letter. Arguments ranged fiercely with the War Office, but I did manage to get each outpost upgraded to sergeant level.

Life in the Aden colony was peaceful in those days, but there were always ongoing skirmishes some 40 miles to the northern areas of the Protectorate in the mountains at the border with Yemen. There was no road, the only approach being by air. Equipment even as large as a jeep could be carried up by freight aircraft, but no kit could ever come back because the runway was too short at that altitude for take-off with a heavy load. The APL provided the military force. I flew there to see the situation for myself from the equipment maintenance point of view, as was my responsibility. Villages were scattered around, their perilous terraced cultivation strips cut into the steep igneous rock hillsides. At twilight all the villagers came outside carrying candles or paraffin lamps and banging pots and pans as they walked around their plots. This was to scare off the locusts, in effect to drive them away to the next village. Next day they were back again and I took a couple of photographs of a locust cloud about 9 ft above my head, so thick with millions of the pests that the sun was blotted out. Day was turned literally into total darkness for 20 minutes; it was quite a biblical scene.

Social life in Aden was entirely artificial. We developed our own circle of friends in the Services, dining out at each others' houses. The evening might also include a few games of Canasta or the like. When it came to our turn, the unique location of our hut on the rock provided great scope for treasure hunt types of party game, as we could hide clues in and around these mysterious tunnels. There was an officers' club located at Tarshine bay nearby where the bathing beach was protected by a shark safety net. The tide was negligible. Small straw-roofed sun shelters called bashas were provided on the beach, but to get to one you had to scamper across the scorching sand at air temperatures above 35°C. The surface temperature of the sand was far higher. Audrey Towers warmed her baby-food tins by burying them in the sand. We swam in the clear water and sunbathed foolishly under the overhead sun. Then we would put on goggles and swim again, under water. In the evening our favourite meal in the beach restaurant was lobster thermidor.

Betty and I attended Christ Church, the garrison church which also served as the parish church for the whole colony. The vicar was Padre John Boatwright, a serving RAF officer. We preferred the 6.30 evensong, hoping the weather might just be a little cooler, but occasionally we attended the family service at 9.30 am. When Padre John found out that Betty and I had not been confirmed, he persuaded us to join the preparation classes he was running for some young service personnel. As a routine, he asked all the candidates for their dates of birth, but when it came to her turn Betty said 'pass!' The big day came when we knelt before the visiting Bishop of Sudan to be confirmed. (Now be honest, how many of you have been confirmed by the Bishop of the Sudan?) Later in 1957, Audrey asked Betty to be godmother at the christening of her second child, Nichola. Even in that heat the ladies had enough style to wear hats and gloves, though not stockings.

Once she had settled in, Betty got a job with the local Water Board, preparing bills from meter readings. Her small income enabled us to buy extras such as a Morphy Richards pop-up toaster (which lasted for over 40 years), a camera, and eventually my gold Omega Seamaster watch, still going well after occasional overhauls down the years. I had already bought a small Austin car before she arrived, which we eventually shipped back to the UK at the end of my tour. It had to be lifted on and off the deck of a freight ship in a sling. Vehicles suffered because of the moist atmosphere and the poor quality of body and chassis metal in those days. Moves were afoot for the local Adenese to take over all the offices of infrastructure, including the Water Board, so Betty eventually was made redundant. Later, she worked for the Red Cross at the hospital in the occupational therapy section.

Our shoddy wooden house on the gun-fort had the tired air of a neglected cricket pavilion. It had a kitchen across one end, main living room and front door in the centre and a bedroom, box room and bathroom at the other end, plus a shallow balcony across the back overlooking the sea. If we ventured nearer to the cliff top, we could look down into the clear water to see large ray wafting along like thin carpets. The water feed pipe came across the top of the barren rock and thus was exposed to the glare of the sun, so there was no need for a boiler to produce hot water. In fact, before we left the house in the morning we ran a full bath, so that by the time we got home it had cooled sufficiently for use. Drying oneself was hardly possible, because the humidity meant that perspiration flowed as fast as you could towel down. Geckos living in the rafters kept moths and other little flying things down to an acceptable level when the ceiling lights were on.

The kitchen was quite small and had only basic equipment. The fridge was one of the old domed-front kind with a lever handle. One day, I was putting a portion of chicken wrapped in foil into the fridge when there was a loud bang and I was thrown violently backwards several feet, crashing painfully against the wall of the kitchen. Unknown to me, the light bulb inside the fridge had been removed, so in fact I had pushed my chicken 'bomb' into contact with the bare socket. Muscular spasms did the rest and I was lucky to have survived both the electric shock and the acrobatics.

On such a barren patch as Aden there was no such thing as local produce. Some fresh items might come in from Sheik Othman, an oasis about 15 miles out across the desert floor to the north. Much more came in on the coastal road from Yemen or by air from the Horn of Africa. Service personnel had the advantage of a NAAFI for branded goods. There was also a frozen food depot along the harbour road selling meat, this being cut rather crudely by band saw. You chose your piece from the right side or the left side of the blade! The side streets in Steamer Point offered a multitude of shops selling anything from cameras to fruit and vegetables. A couple of these streets were given over to Indian tailors, who sat cross-legged on the floor. European ladies would take a picture of their chosen dress cut from a magazine and your tailor would offer a selection of materials, measure up and have the dress ready by the next day. They avoided plain colours because of the perspiration patch.

Fresh fish was always available and it was common to see youths with small hammerhead sharks hanging down their backs as they walked from the beach to the main outlets and hotels. One imported item unfamiliar to westerners was the chewing leaf known as qat, looking like a soft version of a bay leaf, grown in Ethiopia, Somalia, and elsewhere in that area. It came in by air and was quickly sold at the airport in bundles as it had to be fresh to be of any worth. It is said to produce mild euphoria, but it is addictive and can lead to depression. The spittle is a dark green and it is banned in Saudi Arabia and other strict Muslim countries.

On the down side, there was no such thing as a holiday in Aden, as there was nowhere to go. On the up side, a holiday could be taken in Kenya, travelling by East African Airways or even on an indulgence flight, courtesy of the RAF. This meant, space permitting, you paid only £10 per head to cover basic amenities for a flight to say Mumbasa. This is what Betty and I did in 1957. The aircraft on one of these trips was a stripped out bomber used for carrying freight; it had canvas seats alongside the fuselage, no sound insulation. The noise level was abominable. Betty was terrified the whole way!

We had three days on the gleaming coral beach in Mumbasa before taking the East African Railways 1 metre gauge night train to Nairobi, over 5000 ft above sea level. This meant that the track was uphill all the way and the train had to snake its way slowly around countless hairpin bends. The train was pulled by a powerful 59-Class Garratt articulated locomotive, a beautiful machine that has its boiler and firebox slung without wheels between two power units to permit following the constantly winding track. Technically, the wheel arrangement is 4-8-2 + 2-8-4. That means it has no less than 16 driving wheels. Even so, on steeper parts of the route an assist locomotive has to be coupled as a pusher.

On arrival in Nairobi we stayed at the luxurious Norfolk hotel, an old style colonial building, where the food was the best we have ever had against anywhere else in the world. We hired a Morris Minor car but there was trouble because, although I had my Aden licence, I had forgotten to bring my UK licence. I had to take an emergency driving test around the streets of Nairobi before the car was released to me. We set off on a tour of Kenya, driving north towards the Equator. Our first overnight stop was at the Outspan hotel, jumping off point for the famous

Treetops. Next was a call for lunch at the Equator hotel, located literally on the Equator at Nanyuki and in clear sight of Mount Kenya. We were served the blackest and hottest curry you could imagine. Then it was due west, virtually along the line of the Equator until we reached the village of Nyahururu, one of the highest villages in Kenya. We were close to the spectacular Thomsons Falls.

The accommodation here was in individual timber lodges scattered around the hotel building, a typical sort of time-share complex of its day. In the morning we were amused to see milk delivered in churns carried on a cart drawn by a bullock. All these roads we travelled were no more than red dirt tracks, kept in condition by constant grading. The roads passed near to villages of round straw huts and all the people appeared to be very thin and very tall; 'Jambo' was the universal friendly greeting. At the turn-off to any side track there would be ten to twenty mail boxes on posts, reflecting the many homesteads located along that way. In the open country we could see free-roaming wild life such as giraffe, zebra and exotic birds. The spectacular Thomsons falls were steep and deep and we got the most dramatic view by clambering down the valley side into a seemingly bottomless ravine.

Now it was time to swing to the south. We were then following the line of the Great Rift Valley, that natural gash through the world's surface which runs forever southwards through the Dead Sea. Our destination was Nakuru, on the western edge of Lake Nakuru where from the water's edge we were able to witness the incredible spectacle of thousands of pink flamingos. This is the largest enclosed nature reserve in the whole of Kenya. Finally, back via Naivasha to Nairobi, to stay one night in the less than grand Pacific hotel before our return to Aden on a direct flight from Nairobi airport.

We left Aden on the Oxfordshire in October 1958, via the Red Sea to Suez at the southern end of the Canal. I was able to point out my 1947 camp site to Betty as we passed from one lake into the other at Kabrit Point, where I had made my marathon swim. I am reminded that when large ships passed through the canal their clearance on each side could be measured in inches, so that they would proceed without steerage with a tiny cushion of water at each side. Our first port of call was at Tobruk of wartime reputation, where we were due to pick up a company of soldiers. We anchored outside the wreck-filled harbour while the troops came out on lighters to the ship. The rest of our journey home was without incident. I was posted to Arborfield in a technical writing capacity and we lived among the rhododendron lanes in a hiring in the village of Barkham. It belonged to another officer who let it while he was elsewhere in the world. The house was named 'Birchwood', so the address was 'Birchwood, Bareham Road, Barkham, Berks.'

One of the technical tasks I undertook at Arborfield was to write an article for the REME Journal entitled 'The steering of track-laying fighting vehicles'. In this I set out the principles involved and various methods of controlled steering while delivering full power to both tracks, in such a way that the driver cannot attempt a tight radius turn at top speed, which would result in instability; the gear selection determines the radius of turn which is achieved. It was published in 1960, after I had left the army. What readers at the time would not realize is that I was unable to disclose confidential information on the Merritt-Brown gearbox used in my beloved Centurion. On reading my academic article again recently I found I could hardly understand what I was talking about!

As to personal matters, after 11 years we still had no children. Betty and I both underwent lots of those embarrassing fertility tests which only proved that we were each on a million to one chance against of achieving a pregnancy. We soon started to consider the merits of adoption, though we felt this would not be wise while I was still in the army. Meanwhile I had begun to sense that my army career was losing its job satisfaction, in that I was likely to drift away from real engineering into a world of false vanity. Betty had no wish to be a brigadier's wife. I was grateful for all my experiences as a young officer, but I had no ambition to lead the different life of an older one. We wrestled emotionally with the twin themes of adoption and of leaving the army, both being hard decisions to make. We knew my income would be killed stone dead. I was obliged to make a formal declaration to resign my commission and we finally were out on the streets in the October of 1959.

We had already had interviews with the adoption branch of the Children's Society and the stage was set. During the year I had begun looking for any job which suited my background and I got one interview among others with Temple Press in London, to join the staff of a seriously heavy monthly called 'The Oil Engine & Gas Turbine', the leading UK journal on diesel engines and industrial gas turbines. My qualifications were fine for the job and I started the first week after I left the army. We found a house to buy in Little Chalfont, Buckinghamshire, using my small gratuity to help with the deposit, and for the first time in our lives we were on the housing ladder. The rigid service rules meant that I was not entitled to receive even a smell of a pension. Early in the new year of 1960, we collected our promised 3 month old baby girl from the Children's Society home in East Grinstead. We christened her Joanna Elizabeth and our new life began.

LONDON

We are all born with the same terminal condition called Life, for which there is no known cure; try a dose of faith.

My new routine meant a daily commute into London. The train I caught at Little Chalfont station was drawn by a steam engine which had started its run in Aylesbury. At Rickmansworth this engine was uncoupled and exchanged for an electric 'horse,' which then joined the outer reaches of the London underground system. The new journal job was just up my street, as I got to travel widely to interview senior engineers in many factories around the country. Meanwhile, Betty got on with her new life as a suburban housewife with a baby, shopping locally and meeting other young mothers. Our lovely detached house gave us lots of pleasure in terms of furnishing, decoration and modernising, and the garden was generous in size. Family and friends came to stay with us and we plunged deeply into this new wonderland.

After one year, my editor was retiring and I took over the top job. That improved my salary and I got a company car, the relatively new Austin 1100 with front-wheel drive. Its road holding performance was astounding by the standards of the day. I experimented with driving to work via the Watford bypass and the journey took just as long as the rail alternative, about one hour 20 minutes, but one advantage of having the car was that I could now go directly from home to make my calls.

The Temple Press building – housing about 25 popular journals including Motor, Commercial Motor, Motor Boat and Yachting, and so on – was located in Bowling Green Lane, not far from Holborn. All functions were handled within the one building, from management to editorial offices, composing, printing and binding. My own unit had about five staff. Our material was hand written or typed up by the office typist. After scrutiny by the editor, the draft would be rolled into a canister, slipped into a vacuum tube and whisked away to the hot metal composing room in the basement. After a while the article came back up the tube as a rough print of a column of type known as a galley. Any illustrations would have gone to the block making office, where each picture was scaled to size and a master prepared on a block of wood. Our next job was to assemble the galley proofs and block prints into the page layout and again vacuumed to the composing room for a page proof to be made up. We would now carry out final adjustments, spell checks etc. and hence prepare a journal dummy. In the composing room all the typesetting had to pass through the hands of the 'readers', a small team of specialists who had final control in terms of spelling, grammar, house style and quality control in general. As publication day approached the editor would go down to the print room to make final checks of the made up printing plates, referred to as editing on the stone. I quickly learned to read typeset material right to left, upside down.

One of my first appointments was to visit the Fylingdales early warning station then under construction on the North York Moors, characterised at the time by its large 'golf-ball' domes, which in fact were merely weather shields over the rotating aerials. My journal's interest lay in the electricity-generating power house which held no less than nine identical diesel-engine driven generators needed to ensure an uninterrupted power supply in the event of a breakdown of the national grid. Two on automatic standby would be running on no load at full speed, ready for instant duty; two more running on idle; two available for start-up at short notice; one or two could be undergoing maintenance and so on, right down to a standby starter to the starter etc. *ad infinitum*; a fine example of several belts and braces. This was a good technical story for me to write up and I can say that I knew Fylingdales long before any of the technicians who manned that installation. In later years, in fact from 1980 onwards, none of my friends in that whole area have ever known of my personal involvement in Fylingdales.

But my most memorable technical assignment was to write about the new diesel locomotives powering the latest trains on the long-distance main lines. I booked a ride in the cab of one of these locomotives, accompanied by a British Rail inspector as was the legal requirement. My ride north started on the 9.00 am out of King's Cross to Darlington and apart from my technical duties I enjoyed this new experience of flying along at the nose end of a fast train. We got off at Darlington and waited on the platform for a lift on the first available train heading back to London, which turned out to be hauled by a standard steam engine of no particular merit, but we clambered onto the footplate. At Doncaster there was a delay, as that engine had reached the limit of its working area and was to be exchanged for another engine for the final run to London. Shunting got under way and the replacement loco started to reverse into position. 'Look what you've got', said the inspector, 'it's the one and only Mallard'.

He was not joking, and before long I was on the footplate of the fastest steam locomotive in the world, the beautiful pale blue streamlined Mallard. I could not believe my luck. On either side of the cab were two huge speedometers which I watched as the speed built up from time to time. After the Peterborough stop we set off again and soon entered the famous long straight below Grantham. The speedos crept past the 90 mark until at 99 the inspector smiled and wagged his finger at the driver, who eased her back to 90, the regulation limit at the time. I even threw a few shovels of coal nuts myself. What a day that was for a happy boy.

I interviewed a possible recruit to my staff named Hanuš Šnàbl, who turned out to be one of the many Jewish Czech children who had escaped from Prague to Britain at the outset of the war with the help of Nicholas Winton. Educated in Wales, Hanuš went back to Prague after the war to work as a journalist but the invading communists treated him as a political prisoner and put him to work in a uranium mine. He got the job with me on the strength of his English, his personality and his technical writing skills. In later years both he and his Slovak wife Titania served with the overseas service of the BBC.

Joanna was growing quickly and Betty was soon taking her to nursery school and meeting a new circle of friends. She joined the local Women's Institute and became president after a couple of years. In her first year in office she was the one chosen to go up to Buckingham Palace for the traditional Queen's tea party on the great lawn, along with maybe 4000 others from around the country.

I was now getting more ambitious in my editorial role. For

example I made a tour of France to visit the relevant large factories, at the same time polishing my technical French. The first chief engineer I met in Paris decided I must visit his factory – which we did there and then by driving out to Orly airport, where his company plane was waiting to take us to Saint-Nazaire on the west coast – just like that! That French trip also took me to Mulhouse and Marseilles. This language refresher course was later to stand me in good stead. French engineers thought I hailed from Normandy, which I suppose was a compliment. Mulhouse is near to Basel on the Rhine at the triple border point of France, Germany and Switzerland. Betty and I sometimes took a holiday in Brittany, or in the deep south-west regions below Bordeaux.

Another business trip was to attend the technical Fair in Brno, Czechoslovakia. I paid for Betty to travel with me. We flew to Prague in a Russian twin jet which had its engines tucked in alongside the fuselage, surely the noisiest aeroplane on the planet. The fittings inside this aircraft were more like a Victorian front parlour and the air hostess was built like an Olympic weight lifter. There was worse to come: at Prague we had to board a domestic flight to complete the journey to Brno. Here an air hostess guided us up the steps, but once we were all in she shut the door from the outside and got off. In Brno we were met by my allotted interpreter for the Fair. He was a Dr Zdenèk Pavliček, a company lawyer no less. I suppose his first name translated as Dennis. We have remained friends with him and his wife Marta ever since.

At the fair I visited many of the stands and made notes on any products which involved diesel engine power. Zdenèk was at my side as interpreter where needed, but I could get on quite well with English. My French was also useful with some of the Eastern bloc countries such as Hungary and Romania. Most stands would courteously offer a coffee or a glass of beer to a visitor, but with the Russians it had to be vodka, always from an open bottle locked into its own block of ice in the freezer. One or two tots of that stuff can quickly make your eyes water! I was also approached by a Czech university professor whose full title was Prof. Dr Ing. Jan Žižka. He wanted me to give a talk at his college to a group of his students on the subject of higher education in Britain. With the help of Zdenèk I bluffed my way through that on the following day despite the short notice. As a reward I was given two fine books. The professor then wanted me to put in a good word for him with my UK learned institution. Wheels within wheels again?

Down the years my journal had always produced a respected reference book entitled *The Oil Engine Manual*. During my term of office I decided a new edition was needed and in 1964 we brought out the 7th Edition, edited by yours truly. Now and again one of the leading newspapers would be doing a special edition for some purpose, so on these occasions I would be asked by the relevant editor to contribute a technical article on a specific angle for, say, *The Financial Times* or *The Times*. Such things were always good for kudos. I would also receive invitations to attend special press conferences in the event of some commercial or political occasion. The highlight for me was to meet the Russian astronaut Yuri Gagarin after his historic space flight around the globe.

Stronger business forces were operating inexorably against the future of specialist magazines because manufacturers were amalgamating or being bought up by the giants, automatically reducing advertising base to the detriment of revenue. Temple Press management tried to respond by widening our journal to 'Engine Design & Applications' but the writing was on the wall. It so happened I had planned a 14-day tour of the Swedish factories and in the August of 1965 Betty and I flew to Stockholm, Betty again at our own expense. I was sponsored by Scania Vabis who loaned us an estate version of the Volkswagen Beetle for our personal use. I visited nine diesel engine factories and shipyards in various parts of southern Sweden and was always received with courtesy and generous hospitality. The only company making industrial gas turbines, Stal Laval, was located in a small town called Finspång in the depths of the forests north of Linköping and west of Norrköping, some two hours driving time south of Stockholm. After my interviews, the sales manager of the gas turbine department said, out of the blue: 'Thank you for your visit; would you like to come and work for us?' Just months before my 41st birthday, life was about to begin yet again!

Back home I soon received an invitation to meet the UK director of Stal Laval at his Mayfair office. He was a Swedish aristocrat named Åke von Sydow, brother of a great actor and producer in his day. The deal was soon sealed. We were young and adventurous, Joanna was only six years old and we could sell our house in Little Chalfont at a profit. I bought a new Austin 1100, had it souped up with twin Weber carburettors and away we went; in the January of 1966 we sailed from Harwich to Gothenburg, our modest furnishings in another ship in containers, all bound for this mysterious little town in the Swedish countryside. What could go wrong? Answer: everything! The first ominous warnings came as the ferry noisily cracked its way through thin ice floes in the final approaches to Gothenburg.

SWEDEN

Those who purport to be very clever place a great strain on their modesty.

The journey from Harwich to Gothenburg on the west coast of Sweden took 25 hours. Mistake number one: this was the coldest Swedish winter for decades. Soon after we set off northwards from Gothenburg (driving on the left, as in the UK) the engine of my car started to suffer breathing problems, leading to total shut-down, as the superb downdraught of my new Weber carburettors caused frost build-up in the induction manifold at those low temperatures. I had to stop for many minutes at a time to allow the warmth of the engine to clear the ice foam blockage. Betty and Joanna could not understand such technicalities. Mistake number two: my tyres were not suitable for Sweden in the winter and we slid rather than drove ahead. At one point, when I was taking a slow bend, the car quietly rotated to the other side of the road of its own accord; I had no control at all.

Despite these privations we arrived in Finspång in the small hours of the morning and succeeded in finding the De Geer Hotel; I had learned how to drive a small car with bald tyres on ice, or at least that is what it felt like, even to one who had skated up and down Korea at 30 and 40 below. Our life in Sweden had begun. Within a year I bought a new Renault 16, with five normal tyres, but also five spare wheels with tyres studded for ice driving. Wearing the studs I found one could drive quite normally over packed snow and ice.

Finspång dates back to the 16th century when the difference in level between two lakes was first harnessed to drive water hammers for the production of cannons and cannon balls. This original Royal Ordnance enterprise was managed by the Dutch family De Geer for over 300 years. They also built the castle or mansion with its accompanying orangery in the 17th century; it became the headquarters of Stal Laval and I joined an office in that magnificent building. This was the sales office of the gas turbine company, staffed by six or seven Swedish engineers who spoke quite good English. My job was to rewrite all the large documents in even better technical English when the company was bidding for power station contracts all over the world. I had to pick up the Swedish language as I went along, but I was comfortably joining in at staff meetings within six months. What they wanted was an English qualified engineer who had experience with technical writing and who could speak Swedish. I seemed to fit the bill. Betty and I attended church in the original chapel built into the side of the mansion. The Lutheran style service was not too difficult to follow in Swedish, having a similar structure to the morning service in our Common Prayer Book. Whenever banns were being read, we were taken aback when the second name read out was followed by '... of the same address'.

After a few months in Sweden, we bought a bungalow in a small suburb of Finspång. Joanna had no problem playing with the local children at home and at nursery school and was soon fluent within a childish vocabulary, even helping Betty as her interpreter until the child got fed up with that role. The local children pronounced Joanna as Yon-na. Betty was not doing so well, as the wives of my colleagues came to our house in order to improve their English. On the other hand she could cope with the supermarket, until it came to the check-out. After passing through all the items a cashier would say: *Var det bra så?* This sounded as though one might want to buy an item of underwear, but in fact it meant: 'Was that good so?' in other words implying: 'Will there be anything else?' 'Det är bra tack.' 'Tack!' Tack! 'Tack-tack!' Phew!

Our low profile house was set on top of a large rock outcrop, a series of shallow steps leading up from the road to the centrally placed front door. There was a garage at the side. There was also a rough garden at the rear, backed by a small copse among more houses in a small crescent. It was always a thrill to see the red squirrels scurrying about and there was no shortage of silver birch trees. We were occasionally mystified by a strong humming sound at the back of the bungalow, so one day we stood outside and listened; our telephone cable came from a distant pole to the eaves of our house, and the culprit was a woodpecker hammering away near the base of the pole, causing the cable to vibrate like a string instrument! Beautiful. In the severe winter, with its deep powdery snow and temperatures down to minus 27°C, we learned how to shovel away the snow for access so that I could get away to work by seven in the morning (except when the snow ploughs came by and threw it all back again!). I certainly needed those studded tyres. On leaving work at the end of the day it was nothing to clear away about a foot of snow from the top of the car, but first you had to make sure you really were cleaning your own car! Careless drivers who had pulled on the handbrake when parking soon learned they were frozen on. Many car owners fitted their cars with small petrol-fired heaters which came on automatically 30 minutes before the car was needed.

We would go back to England for holidays by taking the ferry from Gothenburg to Immingham. We usually took the cheaper option of so-called aircraft seats on the upper deck, mainly because Betty has always been liable to motion distress which would have been compounded by going down to a cabin below. For a different kind of holiday, after about three years in Sweden we took a young English woman secretary friend with us on a major trip to the far north of Sweden in midsummer. Travelling gently for 200-250 miles per day it took us four days to reach well above the Arctic Circle, to the mining town of Kiruna, said to be the largest village in Sweden due to its scattered layout. At that latitude there was still plenty of snow even in late June. We had stopped each night in small lodgings. Sweden is a land of trees, lakes and granite rocks. The further north we travelled, the smaller became the fir trees and the silver birch. Eventually it was the fir trees which gave out, whereas the birch survived beyond the snow line in the form of diminishing scrub and bushes. Driving through forest country presented the constant danger of deer, reindeer and elk leaping out across the highway, sometimes causing a catastrophic accident. We were lucky enough not to be tested by such a hazard. In those northern reaches it was quite common to see reindeer wandering freely but they were more frequently in shepherded herds.

In Kiruna we stayed in the midsummer vacant University accommodation blocks. In those northern latitudes at that time of year the greatest problems are the clouds of (benign) mosquitoes and the 'knott', a sort of tiny black gnat which surrounds everyone in aggressive swarms. At about midnight we walked up a convenient slag heap and watched as the sun slowly sank to the horizon travelling left to right as we watched, only to carry on its way without actually setting. We had seen the midnight sun! The next day we set off to cut across the mountains to the Norwegian coast. There was no through road in those days, so we had to drive the car onto a rail flat coupled at the rear of the train. We sat in one of the small wooden carriages as the train slowly wound its way through the beautiful, remote mountains overlooking deep valleys. We stopped for passengers at the frontier railway station of Riksgränsen (State border), at 521 m the highest altitude railway station on that line. Our destination, the port of Narvik on the East coast of Norway, was famous during the war as the terminus of relief convoys to Norway.

To complete our circular route around Scandinavia we drove day after day southwards from Narvik along the Norwegian coastline, sometimes crossing a small fjord on a raft type of ferry, sometimes taking the long route up one side of a fjord and back down the other. We stayed in rental cabins or lodgings as best we could and the people were most hospitable. After Trondheim we cut through to the eastern side of Norway; first to Oslo, capital city of Norway, then into Sweden through Karlstad and Örebro and so to home in Finspång. Fourteen days of unforgettable travel.

Sweden had always had left-hand drive vehicles. However, in 1967 the great changeover took place during the early hours of one Sunday morning after years of preparation: total shutdown for three hours other than emergency vehicles while all the new signage was uncovered, then a restart on the right. There were a few accidents at T-junctions early on, but the nation quickly settled in.

Another formidable expedition test we set ourselves was to drive from Sweden to visit our Czech friends in Brno, this in the days of the Cold War. The great stumbling block ahead was the situation in Berlin and the tricky question of visas for travelling through East Germany and into East Berlin, for which a separate visa was needed. Setting out in the early hours of one morning, we drove to the Swedish port of Trelleborg on the extreme south-east coast, itself a distance of over 300 miles. The only way to obtain visas was from East German officials travelling actually on board the ferry, and for that you had to prove the prepaid booking of your hotel in Berlin, which we had done in our early planning. Sure enough, we got our visas and after a four-hour crossing of the Baltic landed in the East German port of Sassnitz. There was the expected laborious trudge through the formalities of passport and visa checks, with the extra complication of body and vehicle searches. This was not only for contraband, but for unlawful passengers concealed somewhere in or under the car. Then came the drive along broken roads through the bleak, poverty-stricken East German countryside for several hours until we came to the outer ring road of East Berlin. The petrol available en route was about 88-octane and I had to drive with a very gentle foot to avoid the engine pinking. Now came all the same checks again and rigid scrutiny of our documents before we could proceed. The guard eventually waived us on with a cheery 'gute fahrt in Berlin', a sort of 'have a good day' in his language.

And so we arrived in East Berlin, on the other side of the infamous Berlin wall, and found our allotted hotel, having weaved our way through the city ruins. This once grand hotel building was shabby and below one-star standard, but it had to do. It was after midnight and we had not rested for 24 hours. One night in that place was enough for anybody, but before setting off in the morning we went to have a look at the wall from the eastern side, far emptier without the tourists from the western side.

To get on our way we had to pass through a check post once again at the perimeter of Berlin and into East Germany, this time without a hitch. We were directed onto the autobahn towards Dresden and I had assumed there would be a petrol station on the way. That was a mistake. After a while this so-called autobahn dissolved into abandoned road works and we were on minor roads with little sense of direction. Petrol was getting low. I manoeuvred into a village that mercifully had some old hand pumps; unluckily, they were all shut. Locals came up to find out who we were and negotiations began by hand signals. They were fascinated by our young blonde child. It turned out that some of them had permits for small amounts of fuel to be drawn from their private locked pumps, so they ended up sparing us a few litres each and we paid them with a mix of any currencies we were carrying. While we were there, an ominous military personnel carrier came close by, but they ignored us; after profuse thanks to our friendly villagers off we went again, now armed with route instructions for Dresden.

This was the late 1960s, over 20 years after the disgraceful blanket bombing of the beautiful city of Dresden during the war. The place was still in ruins and, this being East Germany, still in abject poverty. In a state of shock and shame we drove through Dresden to the border with what was then Czechoslovakia. The border checks here were the most strict and thorough yet, once again searching for stowaways. We got the all clear; here comes Prague, here is Brno! 800 miles on the clock, two exhausted adults and one child. Our warm reception soon brought back the smiles. Even though our Czech hosts had good jobs and could be considered well off by local standards, their lifestyle was modest to say the least. By prior request Betty brought with her a gift of knitting wools, to the great delight of Marta. We met their son, Jiři (George), about the same age as Joanna.

It was obvious to us as visitors that although our hosts were white collar and well educated – Zdeněk a lawyer and Marta a municipal social worker – they were just as poor as anyone else. Money was of no value in a situation where there was nothing to buy. Nevertheless, the shop fronts proudly displayed their immaculately decorated windows. One special state store accepted only foreign currency, and what was the ultimate luxury that our friends wanted we should buy for them? Lemons!

Our return journey was easier because we knew what to expect: a repeat of the previous week in reverse. Mostly true, but on landing in Sweden we, despite our British passports and local work and residency permits and a child on board, were pulled aside into a secure compound for a complete search of persons and vehicle. The car boot was emptied, seats removed, cases and containers examined. Our Czech friends had sent us off with a basket-weave demijohn full of white wine from their friend's vineyard. Were the customs interested? Oh no, after a brief sniff that was ignored. Turns out they were looking for hidden drugs and we had made the mistake of being the statistical *nth* car coming ashore. What a sad world.

My overseas trips for Stal Laval grew as I gradually moved into an active marketing role. One such journey was to Vienna to pursue a possible sale of emergency gas turbine generating units to a local generating company based in Linz. My host in Vienna was the Austrian rep for our company, who turned out to be one of the landed gentry and whose hobby was bear hunting and the like. On my first evening there we went to the Opera House in Vienna and saw an obscure modern piece from high up in the gods. On the next day he was due to drive me to our potential customer in Linz, a long way along the Danube to the west. He was late picking me up and I was worried about the timing.

He was quite nonchalant as we set off in his car, a shining new BMW 3-litre CSi open tourer, which he drove carefully through the suburbs until we hit the quiet two-lane autobahn – then the atmosphere changed! In spades! Our speed instantly rose to a whispering 100 mph as we seemingly floated along. After a while a large Mercedes saloon overtook us, obviously an insult my friend could not accept, so he wound up the elastic. Ahead was a lone truck which the offending Merc overtook at a reduced speed before again picking up his acceleration. My man matched his every move and continued to accelerate until we sailed past the Merc in silence at an effortless cruise of over 140 mph, by which time the Merc had run out of steam. Honour was served and we arrived in Linz with time to spare for the appointment. By the way, we were too expensive and did not get the order.

Another memorable business trip for me was to Algiers via Paris, flying Air France. The installation site was a gas pipeline pumping station in the Sahara, but the Algerian customer's consultant was based in Paris. I was accompanied by a Swedish engineer competent in French who would speak for the contractual details while I spoke for the engineering. All documents had been compiled in French. So there I was in Paris, an Englishman working for a Swedish company, being cross-examined in French about a complex technical document by a consultant in Paris for a client in Algeria. That was a trilingual trial for me which I relished. We flew on first to Algiers, then by small aircraft to Hassi R'Mel deep in the desert to the site. Yes, we got that order, and I would love to know if my gas turbine pumping station continues to work to this day.

Another time I had a contract to pursue in Tunis with their national power company, which this time did not succeed, but at least I had the privilege of visiting the ancient site of Carthage. One of the problems of fighting for trade with Middle Eastern companies was that competitors from the East European bloc such as Romania, Bulgaria and Hungary would sometimes put in a political bid, so low as to be below even the cost of the raw materials (especially the copper), for some ideological sake. On any trip of this kind, supposing our bid was successful, we would at once telephone the sales director back home: 'John, we got the order!' Response: 'We did? What was wrong with our price?' Thanks very much.

In 1970 some of us went to the International Engineering Exhibition in Brussels where all our major competitors would be showing their latest developments in industrial gas turbines. There was a diversion when we realized that the prototype Concorde was on display at the nearby airport and I went to see this new wonder bird. Some representatives of GEC Gas Turbines were there and in conversation revealed they would be interested in recruiting me. Little wheels started to turn in my head. Back in Sweden, Betty and I began to think seriously about returning to the UK and plans were made. At the end of 1970 I flew on a whistle-stop visit to England, was met at Heathrow by a company car and taken to Whetstone outside Leicester for an interview with Dr Wahib Rizk, MD of GEC Gas Turbines. That settled it. In February we left, just five years after our arrival in Sweden. I continue to receive a small Swedish State pension to this day, its value fluctuating with the exchange rate. After frantic house hunting we bought a cottage in the village of Shearsby outside Leicester and a new life began yet again.

At the speed of light, past, present and future are all with us today.

My new job with GEC was hardly any different from the one I had left behind, namely the preparation of large technical documents required when tendering for industrial gas turbine contracts around the world. My travels now took me more than once to Iraq, mainly to the northern gas fields at Kirkuk but also to the extreme south below Basra. The journey from Baghdad to Kirkuk took over four hours in a ramshackle taxi across the barren landscape. The old Japanese saloon cars plying this trade had elementary air conditioning, which put a high load on the engine and caused serious overheating. We would stop a couple of times at a roadside halt for a cold Coke (kept in an icebox). This was in the early days of the Saddam Hussein regime and there was a lurking danger as we drove through the northern foothills that rebellious Kurds would spring out like highway robbers that were liable to shoot first and ask questions later. In Kirkuk I stayed in a scruffy hotel and next day visited the pipeline company in pursuit of contracts for pumping stations.

The educated oil company engineers were Iraqis, many of whom had been to a university such as Dublin, and more often than not had taken back an Irish wife with them. The families lived in a secure compound, isolated but relatively well off. The most amazing sight I saw around there was a perpetual flame, this being weeping gas from deep in the earth, self-igniting in that heat and impossible to extinguish. The seat of the flame was surrounded by a 25-yard diameter ring of protective rocks. This served as a relief valve, because if it had been snuffed out with say a ton of concrete, it would quickly have burst up afresh elsewhere.

One of my business trips, accompanied by another engineer, was to Tehran, capital of Iran (formerly known to the western world as Persia). Tehran is a city which gives the impression of having been laid out on an enormous flat board which has then been tipped slightly to run downhill from north to south. The more upmarket northern end lies in the foothills and so enjoys a more benign climate compared with the steaming southern districts. Traffic in Tehran is devoid of any kind of discipline other than 'devil take the hindmost'. Give way? You must be joking. Under no circumstances does a driver give way to traffic coming from the right or the left. The resulting chaos at all city centre crossroads rises to the depths of ridiculosity!

Another trip I made with a colleague was to Nigeria in Western Africa to visit an offshore pumping station by the coast of Biafra. This part of the world would later be plunged into a destructive civil war which lasted from 1967 to 1970. In Lagos, we took tea at the house of our company agent, where we met his wife. We said we had to visit the doctor for jabs, and she said: "Quite right too, I am the doctor, so drop your trousers and bend over"! That was for protection against a specific type of hepatitis. To get to Biafra we had first to fly south in a light aircraft to Port Harcourt. This is about as far as any road can go in the direction of the coast, because there is another 30 miles or so of swamp and jungle where it is difficult to distinguish between the land and the sea. The only way to proceed was by helicopter, noisy but thrilling as it flew over those everglades at low altitude. Beyond this point a pipeline system stretched out to deep sea pontoons where tankers could be loaded. I was the one who had calculated the engine sizes, pump sizes and flow rates for that particular contract.

This decade embraced the height of the troubles in Northern Ireland, when anarchists of any persuasion might be tempted to blow up a power station or two, just to cause trouble for the sake of it. The technical answer was for the power companies to prepare mobile power stations which could be moved at short notice to any critical point on a damaged network. GEC spotted this niche market and quickly produced some mobile power stations powered by gas turbines and mounted on large 48-wheel trailers, using mini-size wheels. The multiple axles of the trailer were interconnected so that in order to turn (say left) the foremost trailer axle would swing to the left, the second row less so and so on to the rearmost axles which would swing progressively more to the right, such that all the wheels would describe an arc of a circle. By this means the very large trailer could virtually turn within its own length. The flat platform carrying its turbine and generator load sat above the relatively small wheels. When these mobile power stations were being presented to the Northern Ireland power company I joined the team making the presentation.

The GEC factory and offices in Whetstone had an honourable history of association with gas turbines, because it was here – in engine sheds at a remote part of the factory touching the M1 embankment – that Frank Whittle developed and tested his pioneering jet engines. My daily commute now was through the meandering lanes in the leafy countryside. Other suburbs such as Oadby (where I had long ago met up with the 8th Hussars) were not far away and Shearsby was in easy reach of towns like Lutterworth, Husband's Bosworth and Market Harborough, as well as being handy for the M1.

We had arrived in Shearsby at the beginning of 1971 and before long my mother came to live with us, as my father had died in 1970. The house had a small annexe, converted in the past from a pigsty; we spruced it up and Betty's parents, Sam and Ivy, also came to live with us. What with them, my ageing mother and a difficult teenage daughter, things were getting a bit fraught for Betty. Even so we had lots of good times at that house, friends and family visiting. Sam and Ivy had their golden wedding anniversary, which we catered for with great success. Eight people, each armed with a champagne bottle, lined up on the balcony to fire a coordinated popgun salute.

The village had not more than about 200 residents. There was a pub, a couple of small farms, a church, and a village green. The church congregation numbered hardly more than the PCC itself. The village was too small to have a Parish Council, but was managed legally by a Parish Meeting, of which I took my turn as chairman. My most amusing function was to let the parish fields for grazing rights at a few pounds per year. An auction was conducted on the one minute basis, whereby each bid had a life of one minute. The next bid had to be made within the countdown, otherwise the previous bid had it; there was a lot of gamesmanship going on in that process, with some crafty farmer trying to put in his bid at the last moment so that any challenger didn't have time to come back.

The year after that golden wedding, Betty and I celebrated

our own silver wedding anniversary, this time with a big buffet in our cottage. Then we motored to Scotland for a holiday, stopping overnight in Peebles and then on to Kenmore by Aberfeldy at the head of Loch Tay. This luxury hotel has been formed by linking a string of cottages and lies in an idyllic setting looking down the loch. Nearby was an active salmon leap. The river runs out to Perth and Dundee. On a separate occasion we went to Dundee with Dennis and Doreen and went aboard Captain Scott's Royal Research Ship, *Discovery*.

After having been starved of a piano for many years, I had hired an upright Bechstein for a short while when we lived in Sweden, but it was too expensive for me to purchase. In Shearsby I bought a boudoir grand from a nearby village which was carried to our cottage on the back of a local haulage firm's flat truck. I revived my schoolboy attempts at a Chopin nocturne or two. Eventually we sold it on, just when the Leicester Theatre had advertised for the loan of a piano to be used in a play. We responded, the theatre collected our piano and it was played on stage by Miriam Carlin (for that we got two complimentary tickets). The purchaser of the piano collected their new instrument from the theatre after the performance run.

Bit by bit we felt the restrictions of living in a village with no shops, doctor or other basic amenities. Even the bus ran but once a week. At work I let it be known that I would welcome a transfer if an opening appeared, little suspecting what was to come. The situation in Iraq was becoming ever more unstable and the GEC head office in Mayfair wanted a manager to go out to Iraq to close down all contracts and recover as much of any overdue payments as possible. I was rushed up to London for an interview and that was that. In a nutshell, Betty and I sold up and away we went.

BAGHDAD

Be tolerant, even of intolerance.

Our daughter had left home by then, but there was another matter to sort out: Betty's mother. We took her up to Scarborough with instructions to find a place to live. Go and buy a house if you can. One day she called and said: 'I've found a bungalow?' 'Buy it in our name', we said, and when she got over the shock, that is what she did.

Before long I had travelled via Beirut in Lebanon, then onwards by Iraq Airways to Baghdad. Betty was to follow me a few days later. At the security barrier, a rather large Arab lady was rejected by the electronic gate by a warning beep and she was escorted through for a second attempt. Rejected yet again, she was then examined by hand and allowed to proceed; it appeared that the problem had been the metal in the structure of her corset!

My business base would be the office of the GEC agent in Iraq. Helped by local contacts, we soon found a place for us to rent. It was the home of a schoolteacher who was glad to get a good income while he and his family lived in more humble accommodation further out of town. The bungalow property was built of rendered brick, with faux marble flooring throughout as was typical. There were two rooms on either side of a central hallway, everything on a large scale. The main sitting room on the right was over 30 ft long, this being 'his' room, the other 'her' room on the left being a little smaller, but open to the hall if not divided by screens. This design appeared to reflect the Arab culture. There were two large bedrooms, bathroom and kitchen. An internal but open staircase led to a vast flat roof, where Betty could hang out her laundry. In that hot dry climate, by the time she had pegged out the final garment, the first ones were dry. The whole structure was designed so that a first floor could be added when finances permitted. This was done many years later.

The centre of the roof was penetrated by a rectangular sort of box, standing about 1 m high. In reality it was an air duct leading down to the principal rooms. The box sides consisted of radiators made of fibrous pads held together by wire frames, with water trickling down from the top. Water was pumped up to the top of the radiators by a fish-pond pump in a shallow water tray, controlled by a simple float valve. Air was drawn through the radiators by a large drum fan, the idea being that the moist air would cool the rooms below on the principle of cooling by evaporation. In that dry atmosphere it worked well and it was cheaper to run than air conditioning. Such a system could not work in humid climates such as Basra in the south of the country, or say Aden or Bahrain.

The house was served by two independent water systems, one being raw water taken from the River Tigris which runs through Baghdad, the other being potable water which had been treated. A large valve by the house gate allowed raw water to flow around the front garden in a level channel as and when needed, so providing irrigation to the coarse grass lawn by flooding. The narrow border had some exotic plants and a non-edible banana tree. Where the potable water led into the kitchen, it was the usual practice to fit a sintered stone filter to remove solid impurities. This water was in fact potable in the biological sense, but was liable to contain high amounts of fine solids in suspension. We had to rinse the stone filter core almost every day. The feed to the bathroom was not so protected.

The house was let furnished in a basic way with a very long dining table with chairs, a vast bed and elementary kitchen units, all free standing. Our possessions arrived from the UK in containers overland via Turkey courtesy of Schenckers, experienced continental removers. We set up this new home with our own china, coffee tables, books and so on. Betty then cleaned right through and we felt we had arrived. The owner came to set up the cooling system for us, including fitting new radiators to that unit on the roof. Finally when all was ready we switched on and … disaster! Dust accumulated over many months in the ducting was blown throughout the house and into every nook and cranny. Clouds of dust covered floors, furniture, the lot. Betty cried with despair and anger. The owner dashed away to fetch his cleaning woman, who then went through the place with a wet cloth, but it was a lost cause. Every item of glass and crockery we had cleaned after the unpacking had to be cleaned again.

Over the years, GEC had sold and installed lots of power station equipment and pipeline pumping stations to Iraq. Many of these contracts were still extant, where retention monies were trapped inside the Iraqi bureaucratic maze. Retention money meant that any new system had to run for 12 months before the final 10% payment was released. It was my task to secure these late payments and get the funds into our company bank. All these clients were departments of the Iraqi totalitarian regime, so they always held the upper hand. The problem was that in order to enter Iraq one needed both an entry visa and an exit visa. In my case as a long-term resident I also needed both residential *and* work permits. Obtaining the critical exit visa involved the payment of several layers of bribes (sorry, fees) to a fixer, an agent, a visa clerk or two, and the higher echelons of the customer, who were all in on the racket with Swiss bank accounts. This same customer could (and would) prevaricate by saying that the equipment was not satisfactory because two more nuts and bolts were needed, therefore we will not pay the due balance. There could be no argument, otherwise they would simply withhold the exit visa. Another example of the totalitarian life is that all typewriters had to be registered with Big Brother, including submitting sample sheets of typing, so that the source of any seditious material could be identified.

As a city Baghdad was chaotic, but at least it was safe to go around in, living as the locals did under an oppressive regime. Any local contact of ours would not dare voice a private opinion for fear that someone overhearing would report him to a faceless official. There was no trust, only suspicion and fear. The city infrastructure was primitive: mains cables strung carelessly on poles along the streets, drains were open gullies. Private enterprise was virtually non-existent, beyond small bakeries and street sellers of vegetables. Even they could do no more than sell whatever had come into the country that week as rationed out to them by the government. Restaurants could only offer what had been allowed in, as they had no control over their own food purchases. Menus were therefore very short on variety. Sometimes the waiter would say: 'No flambé tonight, bad men steal spirit to make bombs'. A menu might offer: 'Crum chaps' or 'Chat-o-Brian for two parsons'. No one corrected their English!

The whole of the Iraqi infrastructure being state owned, each branch was entitled S.O. – something or other, meaning State Organization for … whatever. Wicked ex-pats quickly invented some choice if not polite titles! For example, the temperature in Baghdad in high summer easily reached 50°C (122F). Above 50°C, the law allowed state employees to stop work and go home. But standard thermometers do not read above 50°C, so here's the catch: as the temperature was declared by the state bosses, it never exceeded 50, would you believe it? The State Organization for Dodgy Standards, I think.

One of Saddam Hussein's palaces was close to the centre of the city, the entrance being via a road leading off a large traffic island. One day I drove along the highway to pay my first visit to the private residence of the British Consul. At the island I made my turn towards his house as I had been instructed and drove through an imposing open gate which had an empty sentry box at the side. I seemed to be in a large park and realised I had made a mistake, stopped the car and got out. A military scout car came up to me and an Iraqi officer approached me. He spoke in English and asked what I was doing. When he had heard my story he said: 'Was there a sentry on duty at the gate?' I said there was not. He took my business card and then directed me out of the palace grounds. I dare not guess what happened to that sentry.

Although Iraq was a Muslim country it was not exclusively so, unlike say Saudi Arabia. Other religions were tolerated and the importation of alcohol was not illegal. The Sunni sect held the reins of power under the Ba'ath Party, but the oppressed Shiites were in the majority, mainly in the south. They were the ones who traditionally lived in the marshes, later drained dry by Hussein as part of his ethnic cleansing policy. There was only one C of E church in Baghdad, St George's, not far from the British Embassy. The last vicar had long since gone and the church building was in a state of neglect, although there remained one faithful retainer who tried to keep the place tidy. Christian business people passing through Iraq from Europe,

India, Africa, America, and the Far East came together on Sunday to worship in a DIY sort of way, with anyone who felt the urge making an address.

George Bailey – a friend of ours working for another UK contractor – wanted to marry, so his fiancée Claire flew out from England to join him. The marriage ceremony was conducted in the British Embassy by the Deputy Consul, as is allowed under British law. The bride was given away by yours truly acting as proxy father. They remain our good friends to this day. After the service, we followed the local tradition of our convoy of cars driving through the city centre: lights flashing, flags flying and car horns hooting non-stop, the local people making way with good humour. George's company designed and supplied shuttering for concrete structures and was based on the same local agent as myself. Other European, Japanese and American contractors might well have quite a large staff on the ground, in which case they would live in their own self-contained compound complete with families. Their work might be the construction of a hotel, the installation of controlled irrigation schemes over large areas using laser-beam levelling techniques, or perhaps the building of a power generation sub-station.

Saddam Hussain was a dictator who had an iron grip on his totalitarian state. He was fond of scoring political prestige points by arranging conferences of all Middle East Arab states. When that happened, all the main hotels in Baghdad would be commandeered for the distinguished visitors and their entourages, all regular hotel guests being summarily expelled. One such unfortunate was Ray Carr, a British hydraulics engineer working for a French company whom we had met at the club. Betty said he could have our spare room for a couple of weeks until the hotels opened for business again and they arranged a deal whereby Ray would give Betty half of his company's hotel allowance. Betty referred to her share of the bargain as her knicker-leg money; this amicable arrangement helped to pay for our trip to Greece. Ray lived with us for the rest of our stay in Baghdad and he and his wife are friends forever, nowadays resident near Ripon.

I had arranged for most of my salary to be paid by GEC into my UK bank, thus safe from the clutches of the Iraqis. Within

Iraq itself I had sole control of the company money, out of which I could buy a company car, pay rentals, business expenses etc, but beyond that the local currency was of no use. Buying a car was far more difficult than it seems, as there were no sale rooms as such. The trick was to find, at an exorbitant price, a car previously imported (fiddled) by some state official. Bribes again! I got a white Volvo 240 with air conditioning, essential in the scorching heat. We had white linen covers on the seats, just as we had done in Aden.

In the course of my work Betty and I did get to travel to the north or, closer at hand, to Babylon and Ctesiphon. Babylon is a vast site of which only a fraction has been excavated. In comparison with the visual glory of say Greek and Roman ruins, most of what can be seen of Babylon is no more impressive than brickyard rubble, except where ceremonial causeways and main gates etc have been restored. On the other hand, one could not help but stand in awe at the sheer size of this once mighty city, at the mere fact of its former existence. In the far north of Iraq one could find the ruins of Assyrian Nineveh; in the south there is Ur of the Chaldees. Then in the extreme south are the countless date palms below Basra, against the border with Iran. In Basra we even stayed overnight in the dilapidated former Imperial Airways hotel by the Shatt-al-Arab waterway where, in earlier times, flying boats landed on their way to and from the Far East. The Shatt-al-Arab is the mighty estuary formed by the confluence of the Tigris and Euphrates rivers which flow eventually into the Gulf.

The commercial section of the British Embassy was of great help to British interests in arranging contacts and providing market information. One of their staff whom I got to meet was an Iraqi named Samuel Potros, younger than us. We grew friendly with him and his family. We learned they were not actually Arab, but descendants of the ancient Assyrian empire and nowadays practising members of the Eastern Christian church. We visited their humble home situated in a down-town warren of streets, later seen all too often on our TV screens during the closing days of Saddam's reign. They came to our house in Baghdad with their four children. In later years the family escaped individually through Jordan and by devious routes across Russia and Europe, to end up in Sweden where they have now achieved citizenship. I have been to visit them in a suburb of Stockholm on three occasions and one daughter (Nahrain) has been to Scarborough. They took us – with a huge picnic – to a public park 20 miles outside Baghdad. Here was the ancient city of Ctesiphon, the winter capital of the Parthian empire in the 2nd century BC. The hall has the largest single span brick arch in the world, which still stands. An image of this arch was later used on the posters when the Orient Express was extended from Istanbul to Baghdad. I made a sketch.

In our second year in Iraq we decided we would like to take a holiday in Greece, but our Iraqi dinars had no value on the world currency markets. The answer was to buy currency of any sort from visiting business men from say USA, UK, France, Germany and so on, who wanted dinars while they were in Iraq (all illegally of course and usually at punitive rates). Then we had to get exit and entry visas from the immigration office, working through the usual string of insiders who all took their cut. We won these tedious battles eventually and had a good holiday in Athens, Piraeus, Corinth (standing in the forum where St Paul preached) and popular spots like the Parthenon on the Acropolis and the original Olympic stadium.

Mission accomplished, we returned to the UK at the end of 1979. I resigned from GEC and Betty and I began the process of settling in Scarborough, where I wanted to establish myself as a translator of technical documents from Swedish into English.

SCARBOROUGH

The one who never does anything wrong – never does anything.

After various delays Betty and I moved into number 11 Stepney Road, Scarborough in the summer of 1980. I bought a huge Olivetti computer with no screen and a floppy disk of only a few kilobytes, but I had to earn a living. That computer was in the form of a metal desk which took two strong men to lift. I had retained some contacts in Sweden and soon got some good work to do for the Swedish State Power Board and other companies. My method was to send my English text over a modem link at great expense on our telephone line to an office in Stockholm. Transmission was slow and – as there was no broadband – the phone was always engaged and liable to drop the line without warning. Sometimes these jobs needed me to visit Sweden. It was on one of those visits to that office that I first met up with Kjell Lundin (say *Shell Lund-een*). He was a highly respected graphic designer in a partnership of specialists who compiled technical documents and artwork. His wife, Birgit, was a psychotherapist working for the state in addition to having a private consultancy. Kjell and Birgit came over to our diamond wedding celebrations in 2009 and Kjell has always been my friendly consultant on all my translation work.

Meanwhile Betty set up a Bed & Breakfast business so as to supplement our income, very successfully too. I made the small bedroom over the front door into my office and there were four other large bedrooms. We camped in the breakfast kitchen. We had lots of paying guests in the summer months and many family and friends came to visit, including from the USA. Betty's mother came to live with us eventually. For church, we went first to St Saviour's, where Betty's parents had been married; I did a spell there as churchwarden. Later we switched to St Martin's, where I also became a churchwarden. We gave a party to celebrate both our 60th birthdays; we did a trip to Australia and New Zealand; we had holidays in France; we toured England and Scotland; we did a business trip by car to Denmark with the Styches; we had holidays with the grandchildren in the Lake District and Northumbria. That was a quick summary of a hectic life, but the steps at number 11 got steeper, the garden got longer and our hair grew whiter, so at the age of 72 we looked for a possible downsize. Eventually we moved to number 50 Filey Road in April 1998.

At number 11 my translations had kept me busy. I was able to visit Sweden several times. One of my clients was a small shipyard in Öregrund on the Gulf of Bothnia coast north of Stockholm which designed and manufactured 200-seat aluminium catamarans. In order to visit them I drove to Betty's cousin Geoffrey's house on the north side of Leeds, who then took me to Leeds-Bradford airport for an early-morning flight via Heathrow to Stockholm. This method avoided the agony of train, tube, hotel, luggage etc to get to Heathrow. My method with that client was to interview the chief designer, the works foreman and the skilled staff (using Swedish) and from these notes compile operating and maintenance manuals in English, printed in Scarborough.

Usually I had no trouble with payment by the shipyard for my labours, but on one occasion payment was overdue. In pursuit of the money (the account was not disputed) I learned that the shipyard was now owned via a complicated company structure by one Robert Maxwell. I visited the Oxford headquarters of his empire and was received into the inner sanctum of the pompous man himself, who sat behind a very large desk looking down a long table arranged as a T-shaped committee forum. After listening to the basic facts and some idle chatter about my bilingual achievements he told his secretary that I was to be paid immediately. I departed with cheque in hand.

The catamarans had twin hulls supporting the transverse passenger cabin. Each hull housed a diesel engine driving a steerable water jet for propulsion and the ferries could easily cruise smoothly at 40 knots. On my way to Australia on a holiday in March 1986, I took a stop-over in Hong Kong and visited the ferry company that was operating one of 'my' catamarans. I rode with the captain on the bridge of the scheduled service to the former Portuguese colony of Macau, weaving our way between the islands and misty waters like an old black-and-white movie with Peter Lorre and Sydney Greenstreet. While in Macau I sampled a genuine Chinese stir-fry in a rough harbour dive with the dock labourers – now there was a culinary experience to treasure! Then I returned on the next available ferry.

My flight out of Hong Kong was headed for Adelaide, where I was to stay one week with old UK ex-pat friends. While we were flying over Australia, the pilot came on air to say he was banking the plane so that we could all observe Halley's Comet shooting across the sky. This was a once-in-a-lifetime experience. The city of Adelaide did not develop from a penal colony like Sydney, but is built around a protected core of one square mile which is disturbed only by the railway line and main road running across it. My friends took me out to the Barossa Valley to visit one of the many vineyards.

The temperature during my stay in Adelaide hovered around 40°C so most days I walked a few hundred yards to the beach for a swim. Sitting on the beach, gazing south towards Antarctica, I realized with great surprise that the sun was on my back; this is the Southern Hemisphere, where the midday sun is in the north! One day I was taken to the nearby harbour where the Royal Yacht was paying a visit.

After one week in Adelaide I took a 10-hour coach ride to Melbourne, where I had planned to stay for one night with old Aussie acquaintances who had been B&B guests at number 11. When I boarded the coach the driver checked that I was not carrying any fresh fruit or vegetables, nor any open spirit bottles, as these items could not be taken across state boundaries. My host took me out in his very old and very large Mercedes, which wallowed about like a rowboat at sea (his shockers were shot) on the minor roads meandering through a natural forest full of giant tree ferns. He took me to a game reserve to see my first koala bear in its natural surroundings. Wardens were moving koalas from one compound to another by dropping sacks over their heads before gathering them up in their arms. The bad tempered little bears were not pleased.

Next day, I flew to Canberra in Australian Capital Territory to stay a week with our old Aussie pals the Barbers from our Swanage days. Canberra, the national capital, is a purpose-built city founded in 1913. It houses all the foreign embassies, each constructed in the style of their home country. This rather dull diplomatic hub is surrounded by a number of satellite residential suburbs. A neighbour wrangled me a pass to visit the new national parliament, then under construction. I was able to walk the corridors of power and peer into the new debating chambers before the politicians got there. I then had a flight to Cairns on the NE coast of Australia for a few days, for which my brother Tom had provided the additional funds. Cairns is a popular resort with many modern amenities, but it was sad, not to say sickening, to see drunken Aborigines lying around in the streets and shop doorways.

Like any good tourist, I took a catamaran ride out to the Great Barrier Reef, where a trip on a semi-submersible enabled me to view the coral and its marine life in full colour. Another time, I took a day excursion, starting on the old gold prospectors' narrow-gauge mountain railway that climbed via countless hairpin bends to the plateau above. First stop was a self-contained rain forest, created by tall trees surrounding a small lake. Rising moisture condenses in the high canopy and falls back as rain in perpetual motion. Next on this agenda came a coach ride through rich farmland on the high plateau featuring sugar cane and peanut farms. The large peanuts were really delicious, far larger and tastier than I have ever seen elsewhere. Our driver took us to visit a local wonder, supposedly the tallest fig tree in the world (he would say that!). Birds drop fig seeds high up in the tree tops; one seed lodges in a fork and starts to grow, sending out aerial roots which after many years reach the ground, take hold, and there you have a very tall fig tree. The parent tree is eventually throttled to death. Then came the coach driver's favourite tourist joke: how on one occasion he had to stop his coach because a porcupine was squaring up for a fight with a mongoose; the porcupine won on points! Ho ho!

My visit to Australia had started at Heathrow, so I had gone down to London a day or two earlier and my brother had taken me to the airport. On my return to the UK I arrived at Heathrow, passed through luggage clearance and passport control, and emerged into the arrivals hall, looking for Tom and Joyce. They were there all right, but then so was Betty! A marvellous surprise; she had travelled down by train from Scarborough for the purpose.

One of my translation clients was a company near the south coast of Sweden which specialized in dietary fibre products. I translated all the documents needed for their applications for licences to market such products in other countries. This work was technical in a medical rather than an engineering sense, but I suppose my meticulous approach was not inappropriate. I got so enthusiastic about their work I even created a five-language synonym dictionary of all words relevant to their products. In June 1986, they organized an international conference at Helsingor in nearby Denmark and appointed me official translator. I wanted to take Betty with me so that we could also have a holiday, so we arranged for Dorrien and Gordon Styche to join in. Accordingly, we set off in two cars to North Shields for the ferry to Esbjerg in Denmark. From there we travelled across country together. Betty and I attended the formal dinner at the end of the conference, a magnificent affair in a splendid hotel, with dozens of waiters lifting silver domes from the plates in unison. (Danish joke: Why do Tuborg draymen take a lunch break in a Carlsberg tavern? Answer: They don't want to get back to work smelling of beer!)

For my routine visits to this Swedish company, I would fly from Leeds Bradford to Copenhagen, take a train to Helsingor and finally a short ferry ride across a neck of the Kattegat to Helsinborg where I stayed in a hotel. Each day I took a bus ride along the western coast to Höganäs where the factory was located. This is all lovely farming country that has a character quite different from the heavily wooded areas further north. Nevertheless, there can be deep snow in severe winters. In the year 2000, the new 10-mile bridge at the mouth of the Kattegat was opened to connect Malmö with Copenhagen by both rail and road.

In 1989, February/March being the quiet season for B&B, Betty and I went on a most ambitious holiday to Australia and New Zealand. These long-haul flights usually allow for a stop-over, so we elected to take the first three nights in Bangkok. Because our flight plan included an onward leg to New Zealand, one internal flight in Australia was allowed, for which we chose Perth to Adelaide so that we could visit the same friends in Adelaide I had visited some three years earlier. None of this suited Betty, who is not keen on flying, but she took a deep breath because she wanted to *be* in these places, but not to *travel*.

Bangkok is hot, humid and hectic, teeming with people and seemingly full of tuk-tuks – those noisy, smoking three-wheeled motorcycle rickshaws which pollute the air, but get you round town fast. Most of them sport megawatt amplifiers blasting out pop music. The modern hotels are air-conditioned wonders serving beautiful food, but for a closer look at nature we took a long-boat ride on the river. These boats are propelled by an outboard engine mounted at the end of a long pole which is hung over the stern and manoeuvred for steering. Boys and young men swim in the river like little dolphins, popping up suddenly out of nowhere to beg, or to steal anything over the edge of the boat if you are not looking.

From Bangkok we flew to Perth in Western Australia for a one night stop-over, then on to Adelaide to stay with our old friends. The only special day out we had was to the Barossa Valley, centre of the wine producing area, where we sampled the wine on offer. As part of our travel package I had ordered a hire car, which we picked up the day before our departure from Adelaide. Our destination was Canberra, a four-day drive following the route of the Murray river, therefore across mainly flat terrain. Interesting here and there to see miles of drying racks holding large sprays of sultana grape branches hung out to dry. For overnight stops we had no difficulty finding a roadside motel, sometimes with an outdoor pool. After a whole day's driving in temperatures of over 40C, a swim and a cold beer provided great relief. On our third night we came into the township of Wogga Wogga and stayed the night there. Yes, like Timbuktu in the Sahara, the place really does exist. Finally, we travelled into Canberra for nearly two weeks with Peg and Syd.

On Sunday their neighbours took us to their local church, a very modern fan-shaped bungalow design with four radiating aisles. The fact that we were visiting from the UK was announced at the outset. After the service the people sitting behind us asked where we were from. It turned out that the gentleman, whose name was Hammond, not only came from Derby, he had attended Bemrose School in the years between my brother

Tom and me. A coincidence! One day, Peg drove us out into the country to visit the site of Australia's largest astronomical telescope. Right on cue, the dome started to rotate and the shutters opened while we watched in amazement.

To hark back to my early days in London, I had at that time met an Australian army Lieutenant, Laurie McDonnell, who had known Peg and Syd of old and who knew of my career. Now, in Canberra, we drove over to pay a social call on Laurie and his wife June, before going on to meet a distant relative of my sister-in-law, Joyce Southerton. Laurie was by then the most senior General in the Australian Army, soon to retire. We are still in touch.

Finally came our time to leave Canberra, so we handed in the car and caught the train to Sydney, from where we were due to depart from Australia. We only had one night in Sydney, but we did get to see the harbour bridge and we made a tour of the unique Opera House inside and out. In the city, I took a ride on the strange monorail that hangs on the sides of the major buildings.

Next stop: Christchurch in the south island of New Zealand. Once again, a hire car was waiting for us and before long we were in our local motel. Christchurch is a delightful throwback to the England of our childhood, even to having a cathedral overlooking the city central square. As Betty was writing our name in the visitors' book, a voice over her shoulder said: 'Scarborough? Do you come from Scarborough?' The upshot was that this person had relatives in Scarborough long given up for lost. Names were exchanged and back home Betty searched the phone book; in the end, two remote branches of that family were happily reunited – another coincidence!

Now came the great drive around the south island, first due south through Canterbury. I can honestly say you cannot have seen so many sheep in your life! Lush fields and mountains were ever closing in from our right. Finally, we had gone far enough south and had to swing to the west, through the endless valleys which would take us from the east coast to the west, after first pausing to witness the first and greatest of the now commonplace bungee jumping platforms.

We were then treated to an example of the magic of nature.

Imagine driving quietly along a flat valley floor between majestic heights, the road ahead gently snaking around the slow curves, until it disappears into the distance. After some fifteen or twenty minutes of this soporific progress, I came to realize that the picture before me did not appear to have altered one bit. The scene ahead was still the same, a winding road snaking through the valley, the distant view quietly coming into focus. Here was a beautiful portrayal of life, the future gently merging into the present before continuing to fade into the past. Between the hills were the most amazing lakes which seemed to shimmer in turquoise, apparently due to the glacial minerals washed down from Mount Cook and the other great mountains. We stayed overnight in a small timeshare type of complex, where the timber lodges were of a tall upturned V construction. Eventually, it was time to head north on the west coast, very sub-tropical in nature. At one point we turned inland for about two miles, stopped, and walked onto the base of a glacier. Palm trees and ice, we could not believe it.

After a final night stop on this west coast, we turned inland to cross the mountain range on our way to Christchurch. The narrow road climbed its way ever higher through the mountain valleys, hairpin after hairpin, always with a frighteningly sheer drop on one side. We came to the notorious Arthur's Pass where the road crossed the neck of the valley, at which point it became isolated on *both* sides until the opposite side of the neck was reached. I stopped in a lay-by at this point in order to summon up my courage before gingerly inching the car across this 200-yard tightrope in the sky. Scary.

A short flight took us directly to Auckland, to be met in by our NZ friends whom we had first met in Sweden. The tourist highlight of our stay in the north island was a visit to Rotorua, famous for its hot springs and geysers. We saw the sulphur pools where a hot geyser would unpredictably spout up here and there with a noisy whoosh. Another aspect of the springs was that in the whole area, steam could be seen weeping out of the ground; hot water came free of charge in Rotorua. We also visited a Maori long house and rubbed noses. I indulged myself with a 30-minute flight from the main lake in a seaplane, a 7 seater Cessna on floats. This took us around the immediate area so that we could look down on the various sulphur pools, but most striking was the site of an enormous hole in the ground where a one cubic mile of rock had exploded into the sky many centuries ago. The sensation of the seaplane scuttering across the water on take-off and landing was similar to driving over a cattle grid at speed.

In the days of Betty's B&B business we had met a couple of Australian ladies who came from the Sunshine Coast area, north of Brisbane, and we had always kept in touch. Now, as we left Auckland, our first stop was in Brisbane from where we hired a car and drove north to Moffat Beach near Caloundra in order to stay with those ladies for about three nights. The drawback was that they would be away; but they had arranged for the neighbours to let us into the house. We drove away from Brisbane quite late at night, phoned ahead to say we would be delayed, and finally arrived in Moffat Beach in the small hours. It seemed as though the whole street had turned out to greet us! During our stay, we enjoyed the beach and the hospitality of our new friends. We even drove off with two of them to a special place, supposedly the biggest ginger farm in the world. Several lines of operators sat trimming and sorting roots of ginger, destined for distribution all around the world to prestigious customers, including Fortnum and Mason.

The holiday was not yet over: we chose a coastal route back to Brisbane so as to visit the local harbour of Scarborough, where we soon found the church, thinking to write our names in the visitors' book. Alas, the church was closed and there was not a soul about. All that remained was the flight back from Brisbane, this time taking in a planned three-night stop-over in Singapore, all part of the original flight package; I had gone ashore there back in 1950 on my way to Korea and had coffee in the famous Raffles hotel. Our initial flight plan had included residence in this hotel, but the airline cancelled that at the last minute because the hotel was due to be rebuilt. Now we found the facade was still standing, but the new hotel was being built behind it and is now one of the most expensive in the world.

My perception of Singapore is that it is sanitized to the point of boredom. The state watches your every move: drop litter and you will be fined; fail to pick up someone else's litter and you will be fined. For those who worship shopping, it is full of shopping malls. If you want to chill out in the evening, try one of the many satay stalls in the open market area. I went to visit the notorious Changi prison, where so many were incarcerated by the Japanese, including my friend Syd Barber whom we had visited in Canberra. I made a sketch of the tiny chapel outside the gates and later sent it to him.

So ended our long tour of Australia and New Zealand and all that was left was the long haul back to the UK, but one more unpleasant surprise was in store. Our scheduled flight was cancelled, because the incoming flight from Sydney was grounded for some reason. We had to fly to Bangkok that evening, check out through passport control and customs late at night when hardly any staff were on duty, doss down in a hotel, and then get up at four in the morning to take the first flight to the UK, having once more checked in. Twelve endless hours in the sky again – in continuous daylight over the Russian steppes – did little to relieve the tedium, but we arrived home safely and thanked our kind neighbour Ellen Nagle in number 13 for looking after our house.

A lot of life was lived in number 11 and is now being lived in number 50 Filey Road, to where we moved in 1999. For example, in 1984 we gave a joint 60th birthday party, insisting on Twenties dress, which was great fun. Some ladies wore genuine garments from the period when we were born. We often went to the Theatre in the Round, both in its old building and in the newly converted Odeon when it was completed. In fact, I was the one who compiled the first mailing list for the theatre on my original computer. No one ever knew that. I joined the art club in the crypt of St Martin's, which helped me to renew my interest in drawing; many of my masterpieces are now with family elsewhere in the world. In 1994 I took over as churchwarden at St Martin's where my major projects included the repair of the tenor bell wheel and clapper with the help of skilled woodworker Ron Stringer. I project-managed the restoration of the Father Willis organ, which cost the church £200 000. I had a running battle with the old gas-fired boiler in the cellar, which was very tricky to start up. Also, there was often a water leak and I frequently was down there for an hour or two in my wellie boots scooping out the flood water with a bucket. The water leak was eventually traced to a cracked joint in the greenhouse pipes in the crawl space underneath the choir vestry. Happy days! In January 2002 I flew to Los Angeles to join in the celebration of Doreen and Dennis's golden wedding.

After a couple of years in number 50, I bought a Clavinova piano, made by Yamaha. In reality this is a superior bit of hi-fi with a full 88-note keyboard. This piano is always in tune and I enjoy the ability to use headphones and play in isolation. Chopin is making a comeback, but I have also had a go at composing simple pieces myself. One of my anthems, entitled *The Gift of Life*, is now in the repertoire of St Martin's and can be sung by the choir during the administration of the elements.

P S :

My memory is so bad I can no longer remember what it is I have forgotten.

There we have it: details of a life full of people, places, experiences and feelings are now exposed for all to see. Any sense of embarrassment is balanced by the relief of writing it down in a presentable form. Inevitably, some anecdotes have been neglected. For example, in our Baghdad days, visiting business men from UK companies could only socialize at the British club. The news soon spread that Betty provided a full English breakfast in our house on Friday mornings, the entry ticket needed being a pack of bacon or sausages purchased en route at the excellent Schipol airport in Holland. We usually had a full house.

We celebrated our Golden wedding in 1999 in our flat by using an outside caterer; for our Diamond wedding in 2009 we gave a party at the Everley hotel in Hackness, just a few miles to the north-west of Scarborough. We were 50 strong for the first event, 65 plus three great-grandchildren for the second – much happiness all round. Also, in 2009 my small front garden won silver gilt in the local 'best kept' competition. In 2010 my level dropped to silver, but in both 2011 and 2012 I hit back with gold; sounds like it is time to retire while I am ahead.

My hobby over the last 25 years has been to translate the works of Albert Engström, Swedish humorist, cartoonist and writer of travelogues. In 1987, I had been to Sweden by ferry in my car and performed my translation of one short story before the annual meeting of the AE society, then visited the author's museum in Grisslehamn on the Gulf of Bothnia coast. In the summer of 2010, I was there again for the 75th birthday of our friend Birgit mentioned earlier, coincidentally on the weekend of the marriage of the Swedish royal princess (for which event I did not have a ticket, which was a shame). This time I called on our ex-Iraq Assyrian friends. My gift to them was a fine stained glass trinket box from the Killerby glass works close to Scarborough and a Chelsea shirt for a teenage grandson of the family, as requested. Life is quieter now. Betty and I confine our travels to the local Yorkshire area. Even so, there never seems to be a minute to spare. May this story run and run!